DIGITAL INK

Writing Killer Fiction in the E-book Age

D1738815

By

Bonnie Hearn Hill

&

Christopher Allan Poe

PRAISE FOR DIGITAL INK

"A go-to Bible for all things writing. This book is packed with clear information, advice, and examples that will transform your novel. Before you publish, read this book!"
-JEN CALONITA, Bestselling author of *SECRETS OF MY HOLLYWOOD LIFE* and the *BELLES* series.

"Digital Ink is a MUST-READ for unpublished authors, as well as those of us who wish to review our craft."
KAT MARTIN, New York Times bestselling author.

"Bonnie Hearn Hill and Christopher Allan Poe remind us of the critical importance of craft in captivating today's reader. A quick and highly recommended read for today's serious writer."
-DORIS BOOTH, Editor-in-Chief, Authorlink

"Using humor and know-how, Hill and Poe will transform the novice and educate advanced novelists."
-NICK BELARDES, Illustrator of New York Times bestselling novel, *WEST OF HERE*

CONTENTS

ACKNOWLEDGMENTS

We are grateful to the following for their encouragement and feedback.

Lawrence Fisher
Dennis Caeton
Angelica Carpenter
Hazel Dixon-Cooper
Elbie Groves
Larry Hill
Brandi Hitt
Genevieve Hinson
Dennis Lewis

INTRODUCTION

DIGITAL MANIA: IT'S ABOUT MORE THAN MARKETING

You're a writer.
You want to be published.
You can be.

It seems awfully simple, but it's the truth. Digital mania is not an overstatement. In late 2007, an earthquake shook the publishing world and its name was Kindle. Two years later, Nook fractured the foundation further. Apple's iPad then sealed the deal by bringing in the casual reader. You may love the idea of e-books, or you may hate it. Either way, these tectonic shifts won't reverse themselves. Just ask the music industry.

Although the changes can feel disorienting, this is actually the most exciting time in publishing since the invention of the Gutenberg press. Self-publishing is no longer a last resort for the desperate. E-book sales are soaring, and we writers now have options.

Put your masterpiece online, read the latest marketing blog, and, at least in theory, you've got as fair a chance at potential buyers as Stephen King. If that's all there were to it, we wouldn't have written this guide. But that isn't all there is to it. Sure, nothing is stopping you from publishing this very minute. Nothing is stopping any of us. In fact, anyone who can write a grocery list is also able to publish his book just like you.

This includes drunken Uncle Bob, with his how-to guide on the perfect technique to hit on college women. Don't forget your coworker, Marjorie, whose debut manuscript involves her protagonist weeping for fifteen pages. Yes, they and everyone else can see their names in lights, millions of us all competing for the same readers. That sense of the competition is why so much of the dialogue about e-books has centered on marketing.

But in the rush of data about electronic books and digital media, crucial information about the craft of writing is missing. Not any longer. By the time you finish reading this, you will know how to write a novel that accomplishes what all fiction must, regardless of genre or format. You will learn how to hook and hold a reader, and you will be able to make your novel stand out in the age of digital mania.

Yes, everyone is talking about marketing e-books and making a fortune. Here's what hasn't been said: You can market your heart out, you can tweet and blog like a hacker on meth, but if you have not written a compelling novel that makes the reader want to put everything else on hold, you're not going to make the sale.

Some supposed experts have actually said that you don't have to be a good writer in order to sell books today. Nonsense. If your novel is terrible, the reader won't finish it. Nor will that person ever again buy anything with your name on it. Not even a six-pack of beer.

In order to succeed, you need more than the marketing plan *du jour*. You need to know how to write fiction. Before anything else, you must master a few key skills. We're not talking about charlatan marketing tricks that might fool a few people into buying once. Don't kid yourself. When the reader is staring at that digital ink on his screen, with thousands of authors at his fingertips, he has neither the time nor the patience for shaky craft.

Don't let that deter you. You'll soon have the power to yank the reader into your fictional world and keep her turning pages. You'll have the confidence to know when your story works and when it is drifting off course. Just as important, you'll know how to navigate the uncertain terrain of today's fast-paced publishing culture.

We've said it once, and it bears repeating.

You're a writer.

You want to be published.

You can be.

You can also write great fiction that holds its own on any platform.

Fiction that makes people care, fiction that is exciting to read, and—okay—fiction that entices the reader to hit that buy button time and again. In short, you can have the writing career you've always dreamed of.

This book will show you how.

CHAPTER ONE

YOUR PROTAGONIST: WHO'S DRIVING YOUR STORY?

Before we take one step forward, let's start with the development of your protagonist, also known as the leading character, hero, or heroine of your story.

This is one of the most important chapters in this book, so don't go skipping ahead looking for shortcuts. There are none. We don't care if you're the mutant hybrid child of Ernest Hemingway and the Dalai Lama. No competent author would ever gloss over the development of her protagonist.

Until you have a strong protagonist, you've got nothing but a daydream that will vanish into thin air the minute you cough. If you get your protagonist wrong, well, you might as well take your ball and go home, because the game is over. Problematic manuscripts almost always begin with a flimsy protagonist.

You might be saying, "I don't need to know my protagonist. He's just like me."

There's no nice way to tell you this, so let's be blunt. You are just not that interesting, at least not enough to be your own protagonist. Nobody is. Creating an engaging character to drive the vehicle of your novel will take more than a glamorized look at your own life. It will take hard work.

Be careful here. Writers trap 101. Once you start exploring your protagonist in depth, or any character for that matter, all sorts of outlandish plot ideas will pop into your mind. They'll whisper in your ear. "What about a blind woman with amnesia? Or an Egyptian relic hidden in the Arctic Circle? Ooh, ooh. What about steampunk werewolves? Wouldn't that be a much better idea to write than this stupid book?"

Do not listen to those voices. Character development is the most difficult part of the writing process. Your mind will almost certainly try to lead you away from doing the real work of writing. It happens to all of us. No one really knows why, but it's probably because character development requires an author to poke around in some uncomfortable places in his unconscious.

In any case, treat those plot voices like squealing pigs. Nothing more. Sure, they'll fuss and they'll snort, but you don't have to pay attention. Scribble that great idea in a sentence—that's one sentence, not two—and shove it in a folder for later. Then, take the time to get to know your protagonist and bring her to life by using the following techniques.

Does your protagonist have the right engine to race?

Have you ever wondered why certain protagonists bring you to tears and pick at your brain long after you've put that book down? Why do some protagonists become ingrained in our collective psyche?

Protagonists are the most important characters in our stories. They are the people to whom we relate. Just like us, they are the engines that drive their stories. They race your plot forward, swerve around obstacles, and yes, sometimes barrel over the antagonists in their paths.

Sometimes the antagonist barrels over them. Is your protagonist a sleek, nitrous-injected Corvette, or is he a Gremlin so meek and sickly, that even you, the author, feel the need to get out and push?

Be honest. Your protagonist has room for improvement, right? Otherwise, you've probably wasted your money on this book. Besides, if you're one of the chosen few golden authors, whose glorious protagonist could never be improved, you've got bigger problems anyway.

All protagonists have room for improvement. Fair enough, but how do we authors beef them up? There are laws of gravity, thermodynamics, and government, but are there rules to help steer great protagonists?

The answer is yes. Let us be clear, though. There are no guarantees that anyone can create those characters that become household names. Scarlet O'Hara. Travis McGee. Lestat. Jason Bourne. Easy Rawlins. Stephanie Plum. Some of that has to do with timing, pixie dust, and whether or not Hollywood signs on.

How would you define the traits of a great protagonist? Intelligent? Warm? Giving? Clever? Brave? Those are perfectly good traits, but they're absolutely optional. If you only have these, you're running the risk of a perfect character. What's wrong with that? Nothing, if you're a fan of unicorns and daisies, but how then do you account for the fact that some of the finest protagonists throughout history have shown signs of selfishness, anger, and jealousy? Hell, Henry DeTamble from *The Time Traveler's Wife* spends most of his days beating up and robbing people. Yet we feel no less for him.

Have you ever known a perfect person or someone who pretends to be? We all have at one time or another.

What happens when you encounter these people in real life? Do you like them? Can you relate to them? Can you stand to spend any time in their presence? Case closed.

If you want to touch hearts and sell books, your protagonist needs only two basic traits. Think for a moment. What two qualities can allow you to forget plot and trust your story with this character you've created? These two. Your character must be proactive, and your character must be sympathetic.

- **Memorable protagonists *protag.***

In other words, they must be proactive. Great protagonists know what they want, and they're willing to go after it with all the resources at their disposal. They protag.

What would've happened in the *Game of Thrones* series if Eddard Stockard had simply decided that he wasn't honor bound to be the Hand of King Robert? No war would've ensued. No conflict. No reason to keep reading.

A proactive character is not a victim. Believe us, victims are no more interesting in fiction than they are in real life. Remember some of those stereotypical and oh-so-sexist romance novels of the seventies where the heroines don't do much more than look beautiful and put themselves in dangerous situations?

"Don't go to the tower room," the hero warns her.

Then at midnight, she sees a light and thinks: *Oh, my. Someone's in the tower room. I think I'll take a look.*

Sure enough, it's the crazy uncle who's been kept there all these years. And now, he has her in his clutches. His bony fingers dig into her throat. The room begins to blur. She can't breathe.

And then...And then...

It's the hero! He rescues her, carries her down the

staircase, and she's a happy camper. Stupid, but happy. Who wants to relate to her?

Today's proactive character can't depend on someone else to rescue her, and she certainly can't be the ditz who goes to the tower room at midnight.

Strong protagonists don't have time to stare into mirrors, describing themselves in bouts of introspective sad-boy life histories. By the way, if you have one of those scenes—and we all have at one point—you have to cut it. Sorry, you just do.

Your character needs a shot of Vitamin B-12, and he may need a solid kick in the ass too. Here's how to get him motivated.

Raise the stakes. Higher stakes are always a great way to propel any protagonist. Is she in danger of losing her job? Make it her house or marriage. We're taught to play nicey-nice in school. Not here. Not on the page, and don't be shy either. This is the time to let your sadistic tendencies soar. Scare your protagonist, taunt and beat her until she has to act.

If his life is on the line, who else is in danger? A bus full of grade-schoolers? Better yet, threaten somebody he loves. You may be a pacifist by nature, but you might not hesitate to pick up a spiked mace if your loved ones were in danger.

Suppose your protagonist is terrified of water. What would make her jump into a lake? Is someone chasing her? Is she trying to save someone? The more you speculate, the more honest your character motivation will be.

Get the clock ticking. When implemented properly, a deadline is an instant tension builder because now your protagonist doesn't just have to deal with antagonists, floods, and well-intentioned mothers-in-law. He must deal with the march of time. Just to be clear, the ticking clock doesn't necessarily have to be a bomb.

"Oh, Lucy. I'd love to sit here and drink wine with you, but if I don't get down to the airport by eight, I'll miss my only chance to see my high school sweetheart before he leaves for India. And he's never coming back ever."

Or:

"I need this report by next Friday, Ella. The guy we're watching is in Baja. Your flight leaves tonight."

Ticking clocks or deadlines are excellent ways to prod your protagonist to action.

If you noticed that both of these previous techniques relate to plot, you're really paying attention. We'll get to more about that in Chapter Eleven, but for now, just know that plot and character are opposite and inseparable sides of the same coin.

• **Memorable protagonists are sympathetic.**

You want your reader to turn pages and cheer your protagonist. Laugh when she flips the tables and cry when she falls short. In order for that to happen, the reader must be able to relate to your character and feel her pain. Only then can the reader truly celebrate her victories as well. In other words, your protagonist needs to be sympathetic or at least empathetic.

Sounds easy enough, right? It's safe to say that an unfeeling tyrant, who marches through the countryside searching for orphans to steal, is not sympathetic. Yet, it's rarely that simple. A protagonist who cares for nothing, who feels nothing, or who robotically floats through his life is just as unsympathetic. We, as readers, just don't care about him.

So how do you make people care? Only by revealing the vulnerable parts of his character, the squishy underbelly that most people try to protect, can we allow the reader to feel for him. Our protagonist must have a hole in his life, and the author must reveal it.

What do we mean by a hole? Maybe Mary had to drop out of college to raise little sis. Unfulfilled dreams are an excellent hole. Or she could be in love with somebody who will never return her feelings, which might remind her of how her father always loved the other sister more. A hole in your life is some missing element that both drives and impedes you. You'd better believe that every person on earth has one.

What's yours? Look around at your friends and family. What are the holes in their lives? What makes them vulnerable? Any person who claims to have it all together, to possess everything he ever wanted is usually concealing the biggest gaping black hole that ever devoured a galaxy.

So what's your protagonist's vulnerability? Well, you say, his wife died, and he replaced her with alcohol. All right, it's a cliché. Not a total deal breaker, but you really need to bring your platinum game. If you think you've got the chops to write a better drunk than Matt Scudder, we suggest you go back and read Lawrence Block again just to be sure. Or take a look at *Jernigan* by David Gates if you haven't read that.

Yes, we know that, post-Scudder, numerous writers have created alcohol-dependent protagonists, both male and female. The field is as crowded as a 12-step meeting. If you think your character explores a new facet of that experience, go for it. No rule of writing is an absolute. But if you just grabbed alcohol or drug addiction because it was the first thought to enter your mind, keep thinking.

Readers are not easily moved by the same tired themes and characters that they read or watched last week. Maybe it's the way we're wired to cope with pain. Whatever the cause, humans tend to develop emotional calluses over scenarios they've experienced before. Unique vulnerabilities, specific to your character, increase the author's odds of slipping through the reader's defense mechanisms. Hit him out of left field before he knows it, and he'll be weeping like a toddler who's just learned there's no Santa Claus.

Lionel Essrog, the protagonist of *Motherless Brooklyn* by Jonathan Lethem, has Tourette's. Not only does this make for some stunning prose on the page, but guess what else it does? Right. It makes him vulnerable. At many times in the novel, the reader knows more than the character. "No, Lionel," you scream. "Don't do that. He's not telling you the truth." Pure pleasure isn't it, when a novel can involve you that deeply.

Remember, your goal is to reveal the deep emotions that we're taught as children to hide. Shame. Longing. Envy. Guilt. Those feelings come without words or a thought process, and with the exception of sociopaths, they are universal to the human condition.

Maybe most readers can't specifically relate to a woman who is fighting to save her childhood plantation during the Civil War, but surely you can relate to the helplessness you felt when you were in danger of losing everything that mattered. Maybe you've never experienced Tourette's, but you can relate to how it feels to hear others laughing at you when they think you're not listening. Your goal is to strike the nerve buried deep within your readers and make them feel your protagonist's pain. Only then will they be able to celebrate her victories as well.

There's a difference between sympathetic and pathetic, a big difference. Sure Mommy didn't love him. Or maybe he's a military man whose wife ran off with another guy. Bottom line: nobody likes a whiner. The hole in his life fuels him, but it should not define him. Whiners bore us at the bar and at the coffee shop, and they bore us in books as well.

We told you how important this chapter was. Please, do not move onto the next ones until you give some time—not to plot—but to character. Yours.

Simply put, great protagonists protag. They go after what they want, regardless of the odds. And they are sympathetic. Period. Those two traits are not up for debate, unless of course you don't really want to entertain or sell books. The next chapter will show you how to bring your protagonist to life by developing an antagonist who will drive her to action.

CHAPTER TWO

YOUR ANTAGONIST: THE BIG BAD

Now that you know how to get or keep your protagonist tuned and revved up, it's time to take a look under the hood of your antagonist. This is the primary villain of your story. The Big Bad.

We've already mentioned that problematic manuscripts usually begin with flimsy protagonists. So what's the second most common problem with novels? Yep, a weak antagonist. Your villain is not exempt from character development just because he does things that make you uncomfortable. In fact, he needs to be as believable as your protagonist, more so even, because his actions will certainly be outside of accepted behavior.

"I'm more likely to lose my temper on a film set than almost anywhere. Often the level of idiocy is so exalted that it's impossible to comprehend." –John Malkovich.

Can't you just hear Malkovich's voice in every word? His tone drips with condescension. No wonder he plays exquisitely evil guys. Clearly, the dark part of his psyche is a welcome friend. As an author, you need to be just as close to your inner Malkovich. You must understand what motivates your antagonist. Live and breathe his desires. Only then, will your reader fear his every move and marvel at his unbelievable cruelty.

In countless workshops and writing groups, we've run into a similar scenario. The author, let's call him Jim, has been paying attention, and his story is just starting to get good. Big Bad's on a killing spree. The protagonist is on the run. But wait a minute. Something's not tracking.

"Hey Jim," we ask the author. "Why did your villain just stab that pedestrian? She posed no threat."

"Because he's evil," Jim replies.

"She wasn't even in his path though. He ran across the street to kill her."

"He did it because he's crazy."

With a human population approaching ten billion, there's no shortage of actual stories of human cruelty to pull from. The ten o'clock news is proof of that. Malevolent behavior can be confusing to understand, so let us explain what bad guys don't do.

They don't break people's hearts for no reason.

They don't kidnap elderly folks for no reason.

And they sure as hell don't kill people for no reason.

Are you starting to see the pattern? Banking tycoon and hated Wall Street giant of his day, JP Morgan said, "A man generally has two reasons for doing a thing. One that sounds good, and the real one."

A great villain usually skips the one that sounds good, but he always has a reason for his dirty deeds, at least in his mind. Justifying your antagonist's actions by saying that he's evil or crazy (or both) is sloppy writing at best. What it really means is that you don't know your character. Evil implies a state of being. We learn the word in the first grade along with good, happy, and sad, and the description usually accompanies stick-figure drawings.

People aren't evil. They're frustrated, angry, jealous,

and hurt. Their desire to inflict pain can be motivated by revenge for past injuries. Their thirst for power can stem from the helplessness they felt as children, but nothing was predetermined at birth. Even "crazy" serial killers have reasons. Some of them involve reenacting their childhood trauma, or even sexual release, but the reasons are there.

So what motivates your antagonist? His abusive stepfather? The girlfriend who packed up and left while he was away? Maybe your protagonist wronged him in some way. When you explore your villain in depth and know what led him into darkness, you open the doors of your mind and let him breathe in the real world, a place where bad decisions have consequences.

Better yet, your reader can relate, at least a bit. We've all made poor choices in life that could have led down a dark spiral. Your reader might even feel a flicker of sympathy for him, until her logical brain steps in and recounts all the other people with similar sad stories, who didn't start slinging dope to school children.

Two more ways to beef up your antagonist
If he's not crazy, and he has to be a real person, how can you take this person and give him a reason for all of the horrible things he's going to do? Here are two techniques.

Place him on a mission.
Stan Lee is widely regarded as the godfather of the modern superhero. He described his antagonist Erik Lensherr—Magneto for the comic book geeks among us—as someone who wasn't a villain. He only wanted to defend mutants. Society was not treating them fairly, so he was going to teach society a lesson.

People justify terrible acts in the name of a cause. They

rationalize and even feel good about their actions. Think of the atrocities committed in the name of religion, nationalism, or the advancement of science. The Crusades and the Tuskegee experiments come to mind. In Rwanda in the early '90s, the Hutu generals believed that cleansing the Tutsi population was a moral imperative. Otherwise, they might not have been able to stomach the millions of bodies left in muddy roadways as they passed.

History books are filled with such stories, which is why it feels real when our antagonists use a cause to justify their actions.

Go beyond pure evil.

Many authors create antagonists who are selfish, greedy, conniving, ruthless. Yet Steve Jobs exhibited at least one of those traits when he created Apple. Does that make him evil?

Every sin and virtue exists somewhere in the spectrum between light and dark. We humans occupy that gray area. All of us. No exceptions.

"Not my little Walter," you might say. "He makes honor roll and donates his time to the Red Cross." We assure you, the sexual depravity that occurs every five seconds in the mind of your teenage son would bleach your roots, and let's not get into how teenage girls treat each other. Shades of gray. This is what it means to be human. Hell, even Gandhi lost his temper a time or two.

Just as perfect protagonists are a problem, so are perfectly heartless antagonists. Always remember that villains are people first and monsters second. Bad guys don't think of themselves as the bad guys. A woman doesn't drain her ex-boyfriend's bank account because she's made out of concentrated evil. More likely, she's been hurt in the past, and she uses that experience to justify her actions. That doesn't mean she's any more likeable, but it does humanize her. What are her positive traits? Better yet, what are her reasons? A character-driven reason for your antagonist's vicious actions will always tilt the balance into dark gray, just enough to make him more believable.

So where does that leave us? The good have flaws, and the bad have reasons. Remember, no one gets up in the morning thinking, "I'm a rotten jerk, and I can't wait to mess up someone's life today."

You want an antagonist, not a caricature, a human being, not a cartoon. In short, you want O'Brien from George Orwell's *1984*, not Lex Luthor from *Superman*. If you give your antagonist reasons, he'll immediately become more real to your reader. That, in itself, makes him scarier. Isn't that what all authors are searching for in their stories? One big giant bad guy to keep your readers up turning pages all night

CHAPTER THREE

ROUND AND FLAT CHARACTERS

We've tackled the most important characters in your novel, your protagonist and antagonist. Both are proactive. Both have strong goals. But are they three-dimensional? Most great characters are.

What does it mean for your characters to be three-dimensional—or round, as some choose to describe it? Let's take a look at your protagonist. Hit us with the facts. Well, you say, he's six-feet tall, with gray hair and piercing eyes. Don't forget the razor-sharp wit.

Congratulations, you've just described Bugs Bunny, and like Bugs, this fictional character is flat. In order to write great fiction, we want our characters round, and we don't mean like the cast of Sir Mix-a-Lot's *Baby Got Back* video.

Flat character Frank loves apple pie because that's the best idea the distracted author could come up with while playing Angry Birds on his iPhone. Round character Lisa uses what's left of the apples from the old tree out back for her pie, even though they're bruised and tasteless, because they remind her of the last day she spent with her brother.

Frank likes Christmas because Jesus and turkey are good things. Lisa lives for Halloween. It's the one perfect day of the year, when she can toss her makeup in the trash, forget who she is, and the paparazzi will never know.

Frank can be exchanged with any other flat character by giving him a haircut and a scar. Lisa could have facial reconstruction, and you'd recognize her on the page. Round characters are one-of-a-kind. Every one of their actions has a unique reason that the reader understands. Each action and reason, each intriguing thought, is an additional stroke of the shading pencil, until your character could never be exchanged with one of the Looney Tunes.

Lisa is just plain more believable because she has solid, character-driven reasons for her actions. Believe us that readers, especially the savvy readers of today, know the difference between flat and round. From novels and movies, to television and video games, people have been swimming in both good and bad stories since birth. Your readers may not know the difference between an adverb and dangling participle, but they can spot a bad story instantly. That usually begins with poor character development.

Just to be clear though, round characters are not an absolute necessity to reach people. Sometimes it's fun to escape into characters that don't make us think, and depth of character has not always been necessary to sell books. Just ask James Bond, although we're not sure that Fleming's agent could have auctioned *Casino Royale* in the digital age.

Flat characters are not the redheaded stepchildren of fiction either. They fill great scenes, make excellent sidekicks, superb comic foils, and they take care of all those necessary jobs such as driving the taxi and delivering the mail. You don't want a three-dimensional taxi driver, or your protagonist will be left speechless in the back seat.

You say your protagonist *is* a three-dimensional taxi driver or mail carrier? That's a different story. Characters in supporting roles need to support, not steal scenes. On the other hand, your protagonist and antagonist should be armed to the teeth in the war to win the reader's heart. That includes nice round features that would bring a tear to Sir Mix-a-Lot's eye and send Bugs Bunny back to the carrot patch.

CHAPTER FOUR

DEEP POINT-OF-VIEW: YOU ARE THE MOVIE

Now that you've spent all that time developing your protagonist, you can move out of the driver's seat and hand over the car keys. You can stop thinking about what you want and trust your character to drive the story. The fastest way to do that is through point-of-view.

To be certain, POV is difficult to understand and even harder to master. It is where most authors struggle. Even veteran writers wrestle with it, which is why POV glitches are responsible for most of the problems in your manuscript.

Book too short? POV. Plot too thin? POV. Problems knowing where to end a scene? POV, honey. Every time.

We can almost hear that collective yawn. You already know all about POV, right? Simply put, it's the perspective from which the author chooses to tell the story. Your first writing class spelled it out. The first craft book you bought nailed it for you. You even did an online search. Maybe the class, the book, or the online search did teach you point-of-view. Perhaps, though, it just introduced you to its definition and not its usage.

You can know what something is and still not understand how to use it. How often in creative writing classes do you learn that some books are written in the second person, "you" narrative mode? But how many times are you told that short of *Bright Lights, Big City* and a few lesser known titles, most books in the second person rarely find a readership, let alone publication? Here's why.

You walk into the room, alone as most are in these often pretentious, second-person narratives. A light illuminates the whiskey bottle on the table. You don't question its presence. You are a whiskey-drinking kind of character, especially on rainy nights such as this one. Oh, it's raining, all right, although you may not have noticed. It was raining that night in Paris as well. You remember the smell of it in her hair, the way her laughter chimed. But that was a long time ago. And this is going to be a very long night.

Do you really want to slog through an entire book in this guy's head? Pretending he is you? Or you are him? Neither do we.

Remember, there's only one rule of writing. There are no rules. *Then We Came to the End*, by Joshua Ferris, is about a group of copywriters and designers at a Chicago ad agency facing layoffs after the dot com bubble bursts. It is told in the collective first person "we." Somebody else could publish a kick-ass second-person novel tomorrow. Somebody could also write a book where it turns out that the protagonist has actually dreamed the whole story, where the protagonist is a cat named Bitsy, or where there's no protagonist at all. The fact is, it probably won't be you. Instead, let's look at how you can take what you already know about point-of-view and go deeper with it.

From first-level to deep POV

Your point-of-view character is the person in whose head you are focusing the scene. When you first figure out how to do this, you're thrilled just to be in someone's head. *She saw. She heard. She thought.* And the wonderful: *She thought to herself.* (To whom else would she be thinking?)

Carol saw the gunman hiding behind the potted fern. He looked like he was staring at her, but she couldn't be sure. She heard his gun cock. What was she going to do?

Okay, this isn't the worst writing on earth. It will get you through high school, but it won't help sell books in the digital age. This is first level POV. Although we get the feeling that we're pretty close to Carol, we aren't experiencing life through her eyes.

As you're able to go deeper into POV and write true character-driven fiction, you don't see the character; you feel the character. In a sense, you become the character. Thus, although the POV character may indeed raise eyebrows, smile, and shrug as we do in real life, he's probably less aware of that and more aware of what he's feeling.

There's nothing all that wrong with:

He saw a shadow move behind the trees.

But with a more focused POV, you get:

A shadow moved behind the trees.

Instead of:

She heard the leaves crunch outside her window.

Focus your POV to:

Leaves crunched outside her window.

These are sensory POVs, and you can do the same tightening with description, backstory, and thoughts. Take a look at this.

He was such a jerk, she thought.

Basic POV. Now, deepen it.

What a jerk.

You are in your character's POV. The reader already knows who is making these observations, because we've chosen our point-of-view character, and we stick with her through the duration of our scene.

Many POV problems occur because the author watches his story take place as if viewing a movie. In deep point-of-view, you are not watching the movie; you are the movie. You are a visceral camera experiencing the character's life moment by moment; just the way you experience your own life.

In real life, you don't see your hair blowing in the breeze. You feel it brush across your face. You are not aware of your eyes widening, only your sense of surprise. The idea is to pull your reader inside the character, and you can't do it with lines such as:

Elizabeth never saw the man creeping up behind her.

She doesn't have eyes in the back of her head. Of course she can't see the man.

Or

The last thing he heard was the crack of the baseball bat against his skull.

Anyone who's been knocked out knows that he usually doesn't find out what hit him until he comes around. Even then, somebody probably has to tell him, and he certainly wouldn't be present enough to know a crack was the last thing he heard.

Or

Little did James know that he would remember this moment the rest of his life.

Don't forget, we're not watching James. We are James. If he has no clue that he'll remember this moment for the rest of his life, how can the reader know?

"Oh," some authors might say. "That's because I'm writing in the omniscient point of view. I'm the eye of God, you see."

God, huh? That's a lot of ego you got there. Before you

start messing around with such fancy maneuvers, first learn deep point-of-view. Doing so will make you a better fiction writer. It will bring the reader closer to your characters, which is what authors should always strive for.

Once you learn to go deep, you can decide whether or not you want to be the eye of God, but you should know that advanced fiction writers rarely use omniscient POV because of its detached nature. Get in one character's head first, experience a scene through him or her, and then you will know if there's anything to be gained by viewing the scene from above. Usually, there isn't.

Some authors feel that as long as they're not writing in the first-person "I," they are entitled to leave the character's head and wander all over the place. Not so. You get to decide if you are going to write in the first-person "I," the third person "he/she," or even the dicey second-person, "you." That's your choice, depending on your genre and the way you want to tell your story. Regardless of which narrative mode you select, you should be firmly imbedded in one character's head. Once there, everything must be filtered through her eyes.

Look at this next example.

The storm raged, blowing her ebony hair back from her face and transforming her fair skin into an eerie mask.

What's wrong with this? It's awful, right, but why? When you find sentences like this in your own writing, try to put them in the first person, and you can see where the problem is.

The storm raged, blowing my ebony hair back from my face and transforming my fair skin to an eerie mask.

No living human in her right mind would ever think that way. It's all description. We are outside the character, observing her as if she were on the screen. Now try this.

The storm raged, and I pulled my coat closer (action) *wondering how I would survive the night* (emotion).

Now, if you prefer, you can go back to the third-person "she."

The storm raged, and she pulled her coat closer, wondering how she would survive the night.

The exposition trap

Regardless of whether you decide on first person or third person, you are inside your character, not outside; you are experiencing the scene, not observing it. And you are well on your way to deep point-of-view. This deep POV will free you from the trap of too much exposition. You've no doubt seen the exposition trap before, when an author stops the story to tell the reader facts about the character and her history that the character would not possibly be thinking at the time.

"But," you say, "my reader needs to really understand why Lorna has sworn off dating truck drivers."

We get that.

"If the reader doesn't understand what happened before with Hank, she'll never be able to relate," you insist.

We get that too. Lorna has baggage. She has history. We call it backstory. You have backstory as well, but you don't ponder it day and night, detail by detail. You already know it. So does Lorna.

She'd never date a truck driver again. Hank had taught her that lesson well—before and after their marriage.

And you stop it there. Don't ramble on about how long they were married, and how Hank cheated on her with her sister down at the old factory that her daddy owned. In reality, we don't sit around and think about the truck drivers of our lives. This isn't a country song. It's deep point-of-view, and the reader believes the voice only if it feels natural, with no author intrusion. Besides, you have an entire book to reveal that information when it comes up.

Multiple POV

There's a reason, especially in these digital times, to keep each scene in one character's point-of-view. As you will see in the next chapter, scenes are goal-based, and the best way to keep your reader glued to your story is to put him in the character's head in a scene. The entire scene, from the moment Joe tries to approach Tina, the bartender, about the murder victim, until she tells him to leave the bar and never return. The best way for the reader to experience Joe's frustration and anguish is to be Joe.

Sometimes, however, you need more than one point-of-view. Suppose Tina is an important character engaged in actions that Joe does not witness? Is it okay to include her point-of-view? Of course, it is, but not in Joe's scene. Repeat: Each scene should be in one character's head and only one character's head.

Before you as much as begin your novel, you should have a good idea of how many point-of-view characters you will need in your story. As a rule, the fewer the better. Do you really need to be in Tina's head, or is that just a sloppy way of handling a twist in the plot? No, you really need her; you're sure of that. Then put her on the list with every other POV character you intend to include.

Then do three things. Make sure that you go into a second character's point-of-view early in your story. This signals your reader that she will be traveling in more than one character's head. Also, make a double drop before you introduce the new point-of-view. Like this.

In other words, hit your "Enter" key twice.

Finally, make sure the first line of the new point-of-view establishes the POV character.

From the bar window, Tina watched Joe walk from the parking lot to his car. He stopped and glared in her direction, as if he could see her.

Here, we know that we're in Tina's POV from the first sentence because she's watching Joe. Also, notice that Joe glares in her direction, but we're in her point-of-view, so we're not sure if he can see her or not.

Multiple points-of-view can save your time and your sanity when you're writing a story with numerous subplots and characters. They can also create more problems than they solve. Here are four pitfalls to avoid.

POV Ping-Pong

When you're writing in more than one character's head, it's easy to slip into head-hopping. Avoid writing scenes like this one.

Lisa glared at Joe. "Don't make me call the bouncer."

She'd be pretty, he thought, if she were not so hostile. "I'm leaving, but not until you tell me what time Karen left here last night."

He had to be bluffing. "I mean it," Lisa said, trying to sound braver than she felt. "Get out of here."

If you're feeling bounced around, it's because you were in both character's points-of-view in this scene. How would Joe know what Lisa is thinking or feeling and vice-versa?

No clear protagonist

Most stories have a clear protagonist, regardless of the number of point-of-view characters they contain. Some authors signal this person by starting and ending the story with his point-of-view. The easiest way is to keep most of the scenes in your main protagonist's POV. If you divide your scenes equally among Lisa, Joe, Pete, and Karen, they'll all be fighting to star in your story. Usually, it's best to choose one, and make sure to give her more scenes.

Too many scenes without dialogue

When you're trying to introduce your reader to a number of point-of-view characters, it's tempting to let the characters think about their lives, the other characters, their problems—and not get around to an actual scene with dialogue. Avoid this temptation, and be sure to develop all of your POV characters before plunking them onto the page.

All characters sound the same.

Lisa's voice is just like Joe's voice, which you easily confuse with the voice of every other POV character in your story. Funny thing. They all sound a lot like the author. Lack of character depth shows up in a hurry when you are using multiple point-of-view. Remember, a character's voice is not just how he speaks in dialogue. In deep POV, his voice also includes the *way* he thinks. Look at this example when aggressive Lisa breaks a plate after an argument with her husband.

"Hey Joe," Lisa said. What the hell was taking him so long? "I need your help with this mess."

Now let's see how timid Lisa would think in the same scenario.

"Hey Joe," Lisa said. She couldn't believe she'd been so clumsy. "I need your help with this mess."

See the difference in Lisa's voice. Same dialogue. Different person. If you can't distinguish her from other point-of-view characters based on her thoughts and speeches, the reader won't be able to either.

Stories with deep point-of-view are the ones that win writing awards and get great reviews. Just as important, they are the stories readers cannot put down. You will know it when you're there. It will be that moment when the movie screen vanishes, and you are looking out at your story world from the eyes of your protagonist. Deep point-of-view: Don't just write about your characters. Become them.

CHAPTER FIVE

CONFLICT: "I WANT A, AND YOU WANT B"

Now that you've learned how to develop characters your reader will either care about or love to hate, you need to know what keeps that same reader turning pages for the entire length of your novel.

Without question, conflict is the best way to keep your reader glued to your story. Sounds easy enough. We all know what conflict is, right? We've seen movies with fistfights and laser beams that evaporate planets. Conflict. Blow some stuff up on the page. Problem solved.

Actually, that couldn't be further from the truth. A novel is not a movie. Flashing glitz and explosions might be fine for the silver screen, but they aren't so great for the written word. For one thing, a novel doesn't get to rely on the crutch of a heart-pumping musical score or tricks of lens flare technology to cover up a bad story. A novel requires true conflict, the kind that can only be created by two characters with opposing goals. So what is true conflict, and how do we create it?

Conflict

Obviously, you can't let your character reach her goal in the first chapter. If so, you'll have Cinderella Goes To The Ball Syndrome. Think about what would happen if Cinderella had asked, "Please can I go to the ball?" and her stepmother had replied, "Sure, Cindy. Take my Neiman's card, and I'll have your sisters finish cleaning your room so you'll have time to shop." Cinderella would go to the ball, and your story would be over on page one.

Nor can you write a novel, as did a well-known college professor, about a man (a college professor) who sits on a camp stool outside his apartment and ponders the meaning of life. Fiction is about people. People with goals. Since they can't reach those goals right away, if ever, you need other characters with different goals. This is the essence of conflict.

Why then are most beginning and some experienced writers afraid of conflict? Much of the reason for resistance—and most writers do resist whether they know it or not—is early programming. We're taught at a young age that conflict is bad. You're supposed to play nice. If you argue, you'll be punished. If you disagree, no one will like you. That might be good advice for a five-year-old— *might* be—but it's not good advice for a writer. Like it or not, these were probably your earliest messages about conflict, yet they have little to do with conflict in fiction.

I want A, and you want B. That's it. That's conflict.

I, the psychologist, want to go out in the rain to meet my distraught client, and you, my husband, want me to stay home where it's safe. I, the teen, want to get out of the house before anyone notices how much makeup I'm wearing, and you, my mom, want to find out where I'm going. I, your friend, want you to notice how much you're drinking tonight, and you, the vulnerable widow, want to accept a ride home from the guy sitting at the bar.

True conflict requires two characters in your scene with opposing goals. I want A, and you want B. Not a character alone in a room, wrestling with his conscience. Definitely not a character arguing with his dog, who can only bark back at him.

"What's that, Lassie?"

Bark.

"The boat house is on fire?"

Bark. Bark.

Sounds ridiculous, we know, but for the reasons we've already stated, many writers will travel to the edge of their sanity to avoid conflict on the page. Authors in the digital age can't afford to hide from it, so you're going to have to deal with it eventually if you want to have a writing career. We can't stress this enough. Conflict requires at least two humans with opposing goals.

"What if I'm writing about aliens?" you might ask.

Fine. Two sentient beings with opposing goals.

"What about—"

Humans, aliens, artificial intelligences, dragons with vocal abilities, illiterate hillbillies, or any variation thereof, but they must be able to think and speak. Okay, that should be a broad enough description. We hope.

One character wants A, and one character wants B. The scene starts with A's goal, and the conflict—B's goal— kicks in immediately thereafter. That's worth repeating; immediately thereafter. Conflict begins once A states his goal, and B gets in his way because she has her own opposing goal. B doesn't need to be your main antagonist, although she can be.

It sounds easy, but creating strong conflict can be tricky. If you've been in a writing workshop or critique group, you've no doubt seen examples of mind-dulling conflict, where one character is mean for the sake of being mean. You may have written some of those unbelievable exchanges yourself. We have.

"Hey, Gail. Could we have some coffee and talk?"

"I'd rather put pins in my eyes than have coffee with you, Jack."

"But, Gail, we just met. Why do you hate me?"

"Because this is a scene, you idiot, and we need some conflict in it."

This isn't I want A, and you want B. This is I want A, and you're a bitch. Sure, you can put disagreeable people in your scene, if a scene calls for that. But you don't need disagreeable people in order to have conflict. In fact, some of the strongest conflict in fiction comes from friends and family members who only want the other character to be safe. For example, I want to drive home drunk, and you want me to stay the night. Conflict.

Here's something else you don't need. Surface tension.

The door opened, and a fist shot into Junior's face.

This was the first line in a novel we critiqued. What's wrong with it? Did you say that the line didn't hook you? Did you say you don't care about what's happening? You're right. We don't know Junior, do we? So can we possibly care that a fist shoots into his face in the first sentence? Do we care that Junior and the aggressor grunt and slug their way through the first two pages, and that Elizabeth risks her own safety to break up the fight? No. Because we do not know these people, and because what we have just read is not conflict. It is surface tension. It sometimes works for movies. Not so much for novels.

Here's another example. A workshop member we'll call Margaret, was writing a novel about a family on a wagon train. Mother, father, sister, and little Jethro. If she changed one line, we heard it all over again the next week. Finally, someone in class said, "You need conflict, Margaret."

The next week she was back. The wagon train was rolling, rolling, rolling. And then—little Jethro got attacked by a crocodile.

"Why?" we asked.

"You said you wanted some conflict," Margaret replied.

Surface tension. You can slaughter a thousand characters in a single chapter, but that doesn't mean you have conflict. Before you slaughter those characters, put two people in the scene, eye-to-eye. Don't worry about the cast of thousands. They can remain. But those two characters are what the scene and the conflict are really about. Because one wants A, and one wants B. This is what will keep your reader's interest.

For every scene in your book, just ask yourself what your character A wants. Then decide what character B wants.

So why are many writers afraid of writing conflict? Author Diane Roberts explained it to us this way. "When you first told me I needed conflict, I couldn't accept it because I didn't get what you were saying. I couldn't figure out how you could have a fight in every scene. Then I got that conflict isn't a fight. It's just two people who want different things."

Diane's right. That's all it is. Yet she had to struggle to grasp that concept, and so do many talented writers. We have found that those who don't like conflict in their personal lives require more time to understand that it's okay for people, even people who love each other, to have opposing goals. If that's you, give it time. Ask yourself what your protagonist wants in each scene. What does the scene's antagonist want? Forget the shooting fist, little Jethro, and the crocodiles of the world.

I want A, and you want B. We promise conflict will hook your reader, because it asks a question in the back of her mind. Will character A get his way, or will character B get hers? Humans hate unresolved questions. In order to find out what happens, she'll just have to keep reading, won't she? Mwuh ha ha ha. All right, maybe it's not diabolical, but it's definitely useful for writers to understand what readers want.

Who knows, while studying the nature of conflict and how characters react to it, you may even find, as we have, that you're better suited to deal with problems that arise in your own life. That's just an extra perk though, and way too much psychology to attempt here.

Instead, we turn next to dialogue, the best way to build the conflict we've just discussed.

CHAPTER SIX

DIALOGUE: USE IT TO BUILD YOUR CONFLICT

When we speak at writers conferences around the country, we find that most authors feel confident in their ability to write dialogue. After all, this is the one area of the writing craft that people engage in every day. We talk to our spouses and children. We haggle over car prices. Makes sense that this would be the easiest aspect of the writing craft to grasp. If only it were that simple. Dialogue can be deceptive. Just take a look at the following example.

"Hi, how are you?" Jack said.

"Fine," Tony answered. "What's up?"

"I'm on my way to the store to pick up a six-pack. Want to join me?"

"Cool," Tony said. "Let's go."

"Want to catch a game while we're at it?"

Tony shrugged. "Might as well."

Now that wasn't much fun, was it? Yet we've all written dialogue that was just as pathetic. What's wrong with this little exchange? That's right. It's boring. Sure, people really talk this way, but writing great dialogue is not about people talking the way they really do. Dialogue is, well, dialogue.

Writing guru, the late Gary Provost called it, "the chocolate-covered munchies of fiction reading." When you open a book, don't you skim along and then pause when you see those welcoming quotation marks? When you don't see them, don't you kind of wonder if the book is going to be a slow read?

The reason is simple. As we've said in the last chapter, conflict keeps your reader turning pages. What forms the building blocks of conflict? You guessed it. Dialogue, which is why readers naturally seek it out. Therefore, each spoken line, each word, must be chosen with care. Otherwise, your tension crumbles. Your reader will fall asleep on the couch. Or worse, she will put down your book forever.

What dialogue does

- **It moves the story forward**. Good dialogue can advance the story from two lovers determining a best man to calling off the wedding. It can move a scene from a daughter discussing her murdered mother's will with her uncle, to her realization that he is the killer.
- **It reveals character**. As your characters speak, the reader gets to know them. How a character interacts with other characters reveals volumes about who she is. Does your protagonist bark orders at subordinates or beg to get her way? Does she rely on her sexuality?
- **It clarifies your character's goal**. You already know that your protagonist needs a goal in every scene. So does your scene's antagonist. Dialogue is the natural place for the character to say, "I need to go talk to that witness tonight. I'll be back in an hour." Or, "I do love you, but I need some time away from you right now." Scenes are driven by goals, and so is dialogue.
- **It adds tension**. As you've already learned, conflict is simply, "I want A, and you want B." Dialogue is the only way to play out that conflict and come to some resolution between your two characters. It provides tension for the reader.

• **It improves your pace.** On occasion, you'll find a writer whose pace is too fast. His manuscripts usually read like glorified screenplays, where two characters banter back and forth like floating heads without bodies or a world to inhabit. Most of us need to learn how to cut out the fat and tighten our pacing. Goal-driven dialogue can help focus and speed up that scene that's turning into an epic.

What dialogue doesn't do

Dialogue is not an information dump. Once you launch a scene, you need to let it play out, and you shouldn't have long periods of thought between statements.

"Would you pass the butter, honey?"

The SOB had been out all night again, and he smelled like a wine hangover. No question about what he had been doing. Why did Robin allow him to stay? Why couldn't she just confront him? It had probably started back in fifth grade when Jimmy Reynolds had called her Four Eyes because of her thick glasses. Yes, that was it. And then, rotten Eddie in high school, and all of his lies. If only she had…

"I'll tell you what you can do with that butter," she said.

This is not the way to reveal character. When you write dialogue, focus on that, and don't dump your exposition between the lines.

Dialogue is not a day in your character's life.

In the course of your story, your characters are going to have any number of meaningless conversations. Joe might speak to the doorman at his hotel. His wife Helen might have a conversation with the Domino's Pizza delivery guy. Unless she's sleeping with him in exchange for free breadsticks, you probably don't want to record their discussion about his tip. How will you know what to include? Ask yourself: Is this a scene with a strong goal and conflict. If not, paraphrase or omit it.

Helen went to the front door and tipped the delivery kid fifty cents.

One sentence says it all. We know Helen's cheap without having to wade through six lines of useless dialogue. Remember, each line of dialogue should advance the story in some way. If it doesn't, delete it. Trash it. Control-X it. Whatever, just don't make your reader read it.

Dialogue is not a shortcut to explaining backstory.
Some authors call this glitch the "As You Know, Bob" Syndrome.

"As you know, Bob, Dad left the ranch to you when he died."

"And you've hated me ever since then, haven't you, Floyd?"

"That's right, Bob. I've hated you ever since that day five years ago."

Never mind the fact that nobody talks like this, Bob and Floyd would've hashed this out a long time ago. You need to figure out a better way to explain their history to the reader. Instead, consider something like this:

"Why don't you come out to the ranch this weekend," Floyd said. "Sue can't wait to cook for you and the boys."

"Yeah, that's going to happen," Bob told him.

"Don't tell me you're still angry. It's been almost five years."

"I was the one who kept that ranch afloat while Dad was sick. Not you."

Remember, subtlety and insinuation go a long way with backstory, and it will make your dialogue feel more natural.

Dialogue is not played out in phone calls.
Jake's phone rang.

"Hello."

"Hi, Jake. This is Monique."

"Oh, hi, Monique. How are you?"

Unless she says, "I'm outside on your patio, and I'm going to shoot you in the head," this dialogue probably isn't going anyplace. This is a time you should paraphrase and say something like: The phone rang. It was Monique.

Dialogue has no place in an introduction.
Picture Jake and Monique running into each other at the market. Since we need some conflict, let's do it this way.

Monique was with a guy Jake had never seen before.

"Hi, Jake." Monique and the guy approached. "I'd like you to meet Doug. Doug, this is Jake."

"Nice to meet you, Doug," Jake said.

"Nice to meet you too."

Oh, please. This is not dialogue. Let's try it another way.

Jake saw the guy with Monique in the organic food section, but he didn't look like an organic food type in that black leather jacket.

"Hi, Jake." Monique flushed and hurried through the introductions.

The guy grunted and extended a calloused hand. "Nice meeting you, Jack."

"My name's..." Jake began, but they were already walking away.

See the difference?

Dialogue should not be filled with characters repeating each other's names.

How often should you mention names in dialogue?

"Well, I don't know, Doug. What do you think?"

"Even though I just met you, Jake, I don't really like you, but I think, Jake, that I need to remind the reader of that. Don't you, Jake?"

"Perhaps, Doug. But why don't we ask Monique what she thinks?"

"Good idea, Jake. What do you think about what Doug and I are discussing, Monique?"

"Are you speaking to me, Jake?"

"Yes, I am, Monique. About Doug and me."

Think back to your childhood. When did anyone call you by name in a conversation? And when that happened, what was the emotion of the person calling you by name.

"Billy Joe, you get in this house right now."

"Heather, stop fighting with your sister, or you will be grounded for a week."

Just like table salt, using a character's name in dialogue can add flavor to the exchange. Too much, and you can't taste anything else.

The carousel of circuitous dialogue

Good dialogue creates questions in the reader's mind. It makes the reader wonder what will be said next. That means tension—the sense that something else is going on during the dialogue. If the reader doesn't care what happens next, then the dialogue isn't working.

When we first learn about conflict, we can get stuck in the revolving door. We know about "I want A, and you want B," but we don't know how to escalate conflict to the next level. Thus, we get dialogue like this.

"I'm going to the ball with Sir Winston tonight, Robert, and you can't stop me."

"I can stop you, all right. I'm your fiancé, after all."

"I don't care. I'm going with Sir Winston, and I'll explain later."

"And I said you aren't going, Allison."

"I told you I am."

"And I said you can't. I'm your fiancé."

"I'll explain later. I'm going now."

"No, you aren't."

"Yes, I am."

What's happened here? Not much. We have gone from A to B and not a great deal farther. These two twits are on the carousel of circuitous dialogue. Will too. Will not. Will go. Won't go. Squabbling children that they are, they won't hook your reader for long.

Think about yourself, assuming you are over the age of five, that is. When you want A, and another person wants B, what do you do? First you might try to reason. Then you might try to charm the person into your way of thinking. If that fails, and the goal is really important to you, perhaps you'll resort to begging, or even threats, subtle or otherwise.

Your characters should operate in the same way. Instead of did too/did not and can't do/will do, your characters can engage in conflict the way all of us do in real life.

• By trying to reason.
• By begging.
• By making threats.

Real people use dozens of different tactics when trying to win an argument. Get off of that carousel and move deeper into your scene. Take your time with it. Develop the scene by exploring every ploy the two characters can attempt to get their ways.

Use dialogue, don't paraphrase

Your protagonist barely makes it home to his love

interest. Someone tried to run his car off the road. We know that is surface tension and not true conflict, but he doesn't, and he is terrified. Love interest meets him at the door and asks, "What's wrong, Charlie?"

This is not the time for you to write: *Charlie told her about being almost run off the road.*

Do not paraphrase in the middle of a scene. It is lazy writing, and it will jerk your reader right out of the story. Ask yourself why you want to rob the reader of this moment anyway.

Here's the excuse we sometimes hear.

"But I already described the scene with the car trying to run him off the road. Why would I want to tell it again?"

Because, with all due respect, you are the writer. The way your POV character experiences the scene the first time isn't the way he will repeat it to his lover. Maybe he's trying to hide his fear from her. Maybe he is trying to overplay his fear to gain her sympathy. Maybe he isn't even sure what happened back there on the road.

If you know your character, you can have him tell his story to any number of people while keeping it fresh every time. On the other hand, if you are only viewing the scene as you, the writer who wrote it, your limited perspective will drive you to paraphrasing within a scene. You've heard it before. Show, don't tell—especially in dialogue.

CHAPTER SEVEN

DIALOGUE TAGS: "ALL RIGHT," SHE SHRUGGED.

Now that you know the functions of dialogue and what to avoid, it's time you learned how to incorporate it on the page. We can't stress enough how important this chapter is. You want your reader to get lost in your story—to glance up at three a.m., wonder where the night went, and bury her nose right back in your book.

In order to pull this off, you have to make her forget that she's reading. We hesitate to call this state a trance, but we've all felt the pleasure of immersing ourselves completely in a great novel, to the point where nothing else matters. Any number of things can cause a reader to wake from your story, but the quickest way to pull her out is to screw up your dialogue and its tags.

The tags

A dialogue tag is simply a way for the reader to know which character is speaking.

"Gee, Lindy," Roz said. "I wish I could go out with Tony."

"He asked me for your phone number," Lindy said. "So I guess you will be going out with him soon enough."

"He asked for my phone number?" Roz said.

"He sure did," Lindy said. "I guess all of your flirting with him has paid off."

What's wrong with this dialogue? Is it all of those *saids*? They make the dialogue sound wooden, don't they? That's because the author has yet to learn that there is more than one way to tag dialogue. And it's not always *said*.

Traditional tags.

Joe said. Joe asked. Joe replied. Joe shouted. Joe screamed. Joe whispered. You can probably come up with a few more, but you shouldn't try for too many. When your reader is engaged in your story, her eyes glance at these previous dialogue tags, and she stays in her trance. Why does that happen? For the ecaxt smae reaosn yuo can raed tihs sentence.

Your brain processes those previous dialogue tags and assesses their meaning instantly because you've read them so many times in your life. The truth is, your reader is not really reading those dialogue tags. She's scanning the first and last letters of the words. To have her right there in the story, you don't want her brain working too hard to decipher the meaning of your dialogue tags. She should be focused on your actual dialogue, which should be strong enough to carry the tag's meaning.

Case and point:

"Will you go out with me?" Joe questioned.

"Never," Deborah refused.

"You're so pretty," Joe complimented.

"Get lost," Deborah commanded.

"Damn," Joe swore.

The Department of Redundancy Department just called. They want their dialogue tags back. You don't need the *questioned, refused, complimented, commanded,* and *swore* tags. The dialogue already makes the meaning clear. Remember, if your dialogue needs a tag to convey its meaning, it's probably not strong enough to be in your manuscript. The tags are primarily there to let the reader know who's talking. That's it.

Emotion tags

There's another problem with the scene we just showed you between Joe and Deborah. We don't know who our POV character is. Right now, we are just watching the scene as if it is taking place on a movie screen. Using an emotion tag allows you to remind your reader of the POV character, which will bring your reader closer to the scene. It also offers you variety from all of those *saids*.

"This is the way you use an emotion as a tag." The teacher was as bossy as ever.

Character A speaks, and then that speech is followed by an emotion by either Character A or Character B.

Joe's POV. "Will you go out with me?" Deborah shook her head slowly, and he knew he had gone too far.

"I'm sorry, Joe. I really can't."

Deborah's POV. "Will you go out with me?" Joe's hopeful expression made her want to cry, but Deborah was tough. She had to be.

"I'm sorry, Joe. I really can't."

Emotion tags don't just clarify who's speaking without using *said*. They bring your reader inside the emotional headspace of your characters. In essence, they help your reader become the movie.

Action tags

Also known as a beat, this is simply a way to avoid having too many *saids* by adding an action.

"Actions speak louder than words." He punched the last keystroke into his laptop. "We're finished here."

Or:

"This is the way you incorporate a beat as a tag." She pointed at the blackboard.

Notice that we didn't say,

"This is the way you incorporate a beat as a tag," she said and pointed at the blackboard.

Here, we've added two additional words with no extra meaning, *said and*.

Or worse:

"This is how you incorporate a beat as a tag," she said as she pointed at the blackboard.

Three extra words. *Said as she* adds nothing to the meaning of this sentence. We're really starting to get sleepy now.

Also, notice that we didn't say: She pointed at the blackboard defiantly.

Adverbs tell. Great, organic dialogue shows. Yet every part of speech has a purpose. In the case of adverbs, it's usually to explain something that may not be clear in the dialogue alone.

Take for instance:

"Go to hell," Deborah said angrily. Just like the dialogue tags above, this is another example of redundant language. It's clear that she's angry from the dialogue. Don't tire your reader out with extra words. Look at the next example, though.

"Go to hell," Deborah said sweetly. In this situation, you need the adverb, sweetly, because it's not what the reader expects.

Tagging emotions and actions

Emotions and actions are not true dialogue tags, and they do not require commas before the closing quote mark.

"It's good to see you." She hoped he was too drunk to know she was lying.

"Will you go out with me?" He reached for her hand.

"All right." She shrugged.

Now go back and tell us what's wrong with the title of this chapter.

Smiles, shrugs, and other mindless gestures

Action tags needs to be organic to the scene. Otherwise, you'll fill up your page with useless gestures that don't push the story forward. When an actor in a play performs some unrelated activity for dramatic effect, it's called stage business. That's what we call it when you litter a scene with too many meaningless gestures.

Your character is in the middle of his scene. You need an action to break up your *said*s, so you keep him busy with mundane gestures. He shrugs and nods. Don't forget his award-winning laugh, which he pulls out every other paragraph. He might even go to the refrigerator, grab a Pepsi, and sit back down. Unless he's a diabetic with low blood sugar, we don't care what sugary drink he's guzzling.

You'll always recognize stage business because it reveals nothing about your character. Nor does it push your scene forward. Here's an example.

"Where are you going?" Juan turned to Linda.

"What does it matter to you?" She frowned.

"I need you to pick up some batteries." He heaved a heavy sigh. "The remote's almost dead."

"Fine." She opened the door with her right hand and left. This time, she was never coming back.

There are a bunch of useless actions connected to the dialogue, but they do nothing for the scene. Instead consider:

"Where are you going?" Juan didn't look back at Linda as he turned on the television. Football again. Of course.

"What does it matter to you?" She opened his front door, maybe for the last time.

"I need you to pick up some batteries. The remote's almost dead."

"Fine." What nerve. Even as she was leaving him for good, he still sat clueless, twirling that stupid remote in his sausage fingers.

See how each of their actions relates to the dialogue and their scene goal in some way. He doesn't even bother to look at her. Their relationship has clearly lost its luster. She opens the door to leave him, maybe for the last time. He's twirling her pet peeve, that television remote, reminding her that breaking it off is the right move.

Action tags are great for fiction. Stage business is not. If Mandy is arguing with her mother about the new guy she's dating, maybe she's putting on makeup for her date. Or dressing in clothes that are way too revealing. If possible, always pick an action relevant to your character's personality, her scene goal, or the dialogue it's connected to. Then you'll never again have to worry about stage business cluttering up your manuscript.

Fat dialogue

We authors want our manuscripts lean and fit, which means we must always be searching for fat to trim. Redundant sentences, unnecessary adjectives, or dull adverbs will only serve to tire your reader.

Your dialogue is no exception. What's worse is that it loves to fatten up and fill the page with its unhealthy bulge.

It knows it shouldn't indulge in more sentences, but it just can't help itself. This is why you must be vigilant.

For instance:

"Where do you think you're going?" Juan asked.

"I already told you that I have to go head back to the office today," Linda said. "You'd know that if you ever listened to me. Charlotte's waiting for those reports, and I have to get my car smogged for the DMV registration. Not only that, but I have a doctor's appointment because my birth control prescription just ran out."

Sure, some couples talk this way, but it doesn't make good dialogue. If your dialogue paragraph is getting pudgy, put that baby on the treadmill and trim it down. Cut all unnecessary words. Better yet, keep it focused to the character's scene goal. Usually, a few sentences will do.

"Where do you think you're going," Juan asked.

"I already told you. I have a doctor's appointment." Linda hoped he wouldn't notice the time. "Don't wait up."

Some authors try to make their dialogue appear more slender by breaking a long speech into different paragraphs. That won't work. Each time a new character speaks, that entire speech must be in one paragraph. When you see the pudge settling in, that's the signal that your dialogue is rapidly becoming monologue.

When authors suffer from fat dialogue, they're either trying to escape conflict that occurs when characters go back and forth, or they think they're cleverly dumping backstory and other facts on the reader without using exposition. Both of these concepts are ridiculous.

1. Any opportunity for conflict in fiction is a gold mine. Don't waste it.

2. Just because you put quote marks around your

information dump doesn't mean it stinks any less, and it sure as hell doesn't make it more interesting to the reader.

We told you how important this chapter was, and now we hope you see why. Dialogue and the tags associated with it are the skeleton of your story. They provide conflict and tone for your scenes. When done well, they reveal backstory and emotion. Treat them with the respect they're due.

Your characters should banter, argue, tease, and interact. How else are you going to create true conflict for your reader?

Now that we've covered all of the basics of character development and dialogue, it's time to get those characters out on the open road, by putting them into scenes that will bring your novel to life.

CHAPTER EIGHT

DON'T BORE US: GET TO THE CHORUS

Have you ever finished a chapter of dense verbiage, only to realize at the bottom of the page that you have no clue what you just read? We have. Many times. We've purposely skimmed pages that looked boring as well to get to the dialogue. Let's be honest. Did *The Lord of the Rings* really need fifty pages of Elven song lyrics? We wouldn't know, because we skipped past those too. Bottom line, it doesn't matter if you're J.R.R. Tolkien, Henry Miller, or Dr. Seuss. Long stretches of exposition just aren't as interesting as well-crafted scenes with conflict.

The reader of today will most likely skip large chunks of exposition intentionally or with a glassy stare. Can you blame him? With no dialogue to break it up, these slabs of print stain the page gray. They make it tough to focus on the words, let alone the story. Even our Kindles feel heavier under the weight of so much digital ink.

When a long section of gray space rears its listless head in our manuscript, it's always because we've failed to set up the scene correctly. In order to keep your readers engaged, you must build your scenes properly and strengthen them in every place possible. Here's how to do it, using the tools we've already discussed, and some new ones as well.

Scene protagonist

Always start by choosing your point-of-view character. Let's say this is Linda's scene. Remember, no head-hopping, Professor X. From this moment until the end of the scene, everything we know, feel, see, hear, taste, smell, and touch is from Linda's perspective. In addition, all details should be filtered through her current emotional state. For example:

Linda walked into the house. Phil was passed out on the couch. An empty bottle of Laphroaig whiskey sat in front of him, staining her oak coffee table with brown rings.

Sure, the POV is correct here, but it's not deep POV. We could easily watch this on a movie screen. Boring. We don't want to watch Linda. We want to *be* her. Instead, consider the following:

Linda walked into the living room and found Phil passed out on the couch again. A bottle of that disgusting Laphroaig sat in front of him. He'd promised he'd quit drinking. Now here he was, back at it, with his empty bottle grinding more brown stains into her oak coffee table.

Adding an emotional attachment doesn't just change what Linda notices and thinks. Your choice of adjectives, verbs, and nouns should shift to accommodate her mood as well. Phil's not just drinking. He's drunk *again*. You've revealed backstory in one word—again—without bringing the scene to a grinding halt. The whiskey bottle isn't empty. It's disgusting, and it isn't just staining the table. It's grinding stains, much like Phil's drinking problem is grinding into her.

Scene goal

Next order of business is to determine Linda's scene goal. To do this, we have to know her current emotional state. Sounds like she wants to cram that whiskey bottle down Phil's throat. Since violence isn't in her character, maybe she just wants him out of her house. Better yet, maybe she has a date with someone new tonight at eight, and the last thing she needs is her drunk ex-husband screwing that up too. Perfect. She wants him gone before Derek arrives. Her goal is motivated by her emotional state, and we've added a ticking clock.

Always remember, scene goal is not what you want for your story, but what your character wants for herself. The best way to know her goal is to understand her and what she's feeling. Her goal should be stated implicitly or explicitly in the first few paragraphs of your scene. That way, your reader will feel the tension and the stakes right from the start.

Also, keep two points in mind when dealing with scene goal.

• **When your character has nothing to lose, your reader has nothing to gain.**

If Linda's scene goal is to floss her teeth, you've got a problem. Despite the looming gingivitis, no one cares if she doesn't attain her goal. When your scene has low stakes, either find a way to ramp them up or cut the scene from your book.

• **Your protagonist's scene goal should relate to her overall story goal.**

Detours and side plots can strengthen your novel, as long as they're still tied in some way to the main plot. If the overall story goal for this book is: Will Linda save her marriage, then we're on point. If it's: Will Linda stop the nuclear detonation sequence, then we're pushing it by including this scene.

Scene antagonist

By definition, every true scene requires an antagonist. Otherwise, you're not really writing a scene, but rather telling about an event.

Events read like high school history books, complete with dates and tedious details, where somebody long dead said something about someone. You fell asleep in Mr. Jenkins' third-period history. Your reader will fall asleep too if you fill your novel with events.

We'll get to more about scenes and events when we discuss exposition later in this chapter, but for now, just know that the primary difference is that a scene requires an antagonist. This character doesn't necessarily need to be your primary villain, and he doesn't even have to be mean-spirited for that matter.

Life is full of caring scene antagonists. The head of your PTA might love to give helpful tips for you to become a better parent, or your boss might be a first-rate douche bag. That doesn't make him evil. Your sister could be a bible-thumping bully. That doesn't mean she loves you any less.

In real life, most of our conflict comes from well-intentioned friends and family. Your characters are no different.

For simplicity, Phil the drunk is an obvious choice for our scene antagonist. Now we need to know what he wants. Most alcoholics have a consistent goal. Booze. He wants more. Again, notice that he isn't evil. Selfish, yes, and some would argue ill, but his goal here isn't to hurt Linda. She just happens to be less important than his whiskey.

Conflict

Now that we have two characters with opposing goals,

we have the building blocks of a great scene. Remember, although **Linda wants A, and Phil doesn't want A** can work, scenes are usually stronger when your scene protagonist and antagonist have different and opposing goals.

Linda wants A. Phil wants B.

We know Linda wants Phil out of the house before her date shows up. Phil wants her to head down to the store for some Bud Light, because beer will help him sober up enough to drive home. Big-time conflict.

The proactive protagonist

As you learned in Chapter One, great protagonists protag. Throughout the course of your scene, make sure your protagonist asks, pushes, begs, reasons, teases, and threatens—whatever it takes within the boundaries of her character—until she either gets her goal or realizes that it's never going to happen.

Keep in mind, unless you're dealing with a hormonal teenager, no one begs, and begs, and begs to get her way. Nor does she threaten and threaten some more. Great scenes usually involve your protagonist sparring with your scene antagonist, using a flurry of different assaults.

Maybe she asks nicely first, but he refuses. Time to bat her eyelashes a bit, but uh oh, your male antagonist is gay. Will she try to reason with him? Or does she have anything to trade? When one avenue closes off for your protagonist, make sure she investigates different ones, which your antagonist will be forced to counter. Back and forth they'll go, until they reach a resolution.

It should be noted that threats of gunplay or physical violence are almost always a scene ender. Otherwise, you'll create credibility problems.

"Get out of my house." Linda pulled out her Beretta and aimed it at Phil's face.

"This is my house too," he shouted. "We're still married."

"Don't you test me. Get out."

"I dare you to shoot," he said.

"Say your prayers, muchacho." She shoved the gun under his chin.

"Wait. Wait." Phil wiped the tears from his eyes. "I'll go for now, but you'll be sorry."

Phil is right. We will all be very sorry if we have to read one more word of this. Aside from the terrible writing, anyone who's stared down the barrel of a gun knows that it's not the moment to find the brass balls he's always wanted.

Also, a gun is a gun. Shoving one underneath somebody's chin is as threatening as pointing it at his forehead. Know that if your character is going to pull a gun or break some fingers, there's no room left for escalation, short of murder. That's why it's usually best to go for the physical threats last, if at all.

Setting

Whenever possible, you should always spice up your scene's location. Unless a naked clown is dancing on the pool table, descriptions of your local bar just don't pop off the page. If your scene is in a restaurant, coffee shop, or some other mundane location, put it on a ski slope or on a sailboat. If it takes place at a bar, move it to a factory that produces frozen enchiladas.

Trust us, your reader will thank you.

Also, phones are necessary in real life, but they make terrible scenes, because you're left with nothing to describe but the digitized tone of somebody's voice. As you've already learned, if you need a phone call, make it short. Two or three sentences. Better yet, paraphrase it and have your characters meet somewhere.

She called John and asked him to meet her down at Fisherman's Wharf. Two hours later, he arrived just as the setting sun sprayed flecks of golden light across the ocean's low tide.

Now we're hooked up with a cool setting, where both of our characters can truly interact with each other and the world around them.

Resolution

Any scene should be resolved when your protagonist either attains her scene goal or doesn't attain her scene goal. Did Linda kick that freeloading bum off her couch before her date arrived, or didn't she?

Although that may seem simplistic, it's not. Any scene can produce infinite variations of the outcome. Maybe Linda does kick him out just as her new date arrives. Awkward. Maybe Phil promises he'll walk home, but he ends up with a DUI instead. Or maybe she doesn't achieve her goal, and her new date hits it off with Phil over the bottle of wine he just brought.

Anything can happen, but no scene is resolved until we learn whether or not our protagonist achieves her goal, the one stated implicitly or explicitly at the outset of your scene.

During the course of a scene, your protagonist may realize that she was initially wrong, and her scene goal may shift accordingly. In those circumstances, her new scene goal should spring from the logical flow of their argument, and now it needs to resolve before you end the scene. Or in some cases, this new realized goal will set up the following scene.

Also, keep in mind that once we have resolution, our tension disappears, because we have no conflict. At this point, don't drag your scene on. You should quickly begin to set up your next scene, with a new goal that logically concludes from your protagonist's current emotional state.

Scene versus exposition

Earlier in this chapter, we discussed that scenes are preferable to dreaded events, because they build conflict and make your reader want to turn pages. Events are exposition. They should be used as a quick tool when your character needs to get around the neighborhood.

At its core, the theory of scene vs. event goes back to the first rule of writing. Show don't tell. Consider the following example, which occurs in yoga class the day after Linda finds Phil on her couch.

Linda struggled not to fidget while attempting her lotus flower position. Darla sat next to her, legs crossed and arms out, in the pose of serenity. Screw yoga. What Linda really needed was a cigarette. Maybe then she could focus long enough to think of a way to get Jeremy to notice her. Nicorette would have to do. She popped in another piece of gum. After the roller coaster ride with Phil last night, she needed it. God, she couldn't shake that argument. Was this divorce nightmare ever going to end?

Look at the paragraph above. You can feel the weight

of the dense gray type, heavy on our eyelids. *Go to sleep*, it whispers. *There's nothing to see here.*

Sure, Linda told us a bunch of things about herself and her friend, which may or may not be true, but the reader hasn't been given the option to learn anything for himself. Now look at what happens when we reveal the same information in a scene with conflict.

Linda sat with her legs crossed and tried to find her happy place, but it was no good. Wasn't yoga supposed to calm your nerves or something? How was she supposed to get Jeremy, the gorgeous instructor, to notice her if she couldn't even do the easiest position right? She reached down and grabbed her pack of gum.

"What are you doing?" Darla broke away from the serenity of her perfected Lotus Flower position.

"What?" Linda whispered.

"That's like your sixth piece."

"I need to relax."

"You're going to be the first woman in history to OD on Nicorette."

"I know what I'm doing," Linda told her.

"You said the same thing about Phil." Darla snatched the pack from her hand. "How's that going for you?"

"Quiet." Jeremy, the instructor eyed them from his lotus perch on the riser in front of the class.

Great. This was the last thing she needed. To piss off the only cute, available guy in Manhattan. He finally closed his eyes again.

If these two sections were long-distance runners, who do you think would win the race? The first example is trying to sprint across a track of pure gray quicksand. Even though there are more words in example two, it feels shorter because conflict and dialogue push the runner's pace.

In addition, how your characters react to conflict shows the reader everything about them. Linda didn't tell us she was trying to kick the habit. Darla showed us through conflict. In fact, only through scene and conflict, are we allowed to show. Exposition by its very nature is telling.

This doesn't mean that exposition isn't necessary. Certain aspects of scene construction, such as internal thought, can only be expressed through exposition, but you must strike a proper balance. Exposition is one of many ingredients that make your scenes burst alive. It's not the main course.

The most common cause of writing that drags is improper scene setup. Look at your manuscript. Do you have long sections of heavy gray space, or do you have fast-moving scenes with conflict? In the digital age, your readers are integral to your success. They pay you money. Their reviews on Amazon can make or break you. If you want a career in writing, they are the path. Don't bore them. Or as they say in the music business, *Don't bore us. Get to the chorus.* Your scene with conflict is the chorus. Get to it.

Now that we know how to construct scenes, we'll show you how to link the scenes you've just created.

CHAPTER NINE

TRANSITION: YOUR STORY'S TIME MACHINE

You now understand deep point-of-view. You know how to structure a goal-driven scene—the character's goal, not yours. Show-don't-tell is your middle name. You're writing great scene after great scene, but there's still something wrong. Thrilling as they are, those scenes of yours don't seem connected. Reading them is kind of like watching an *I Love Lucy* marathon. Although you might appreciate each show separately, there's no forward movement. Lucy and Desi are the same people in the fifth episode as they are in the fiftieth. It's a series of episodes, not a story. If you write a series of episodes, you won't have a story either. You'll have that untamable monster known as episodic fiction.

Fiction does not consist of scene alone. Maybe you've sensed that in your own work. You have dozens of great scenes, but they don't seem to connect. You need a way to link them, to move from one place to another, one day to another, one year, one decade to another. Simply put, you need a time machine. We aren't talking about the DeLorean from *Back to the Future*. The device you need is a tool to seamlessly connect the great scenes in your book to keep them from being isolated, episodic incidents.

Enter transition. As is the case with most vehicles, your time machine has an accelerator, and it has a brake.

The accelerator is emotion. It pushes you from one scene to the next. What is the emotional state of your viewpoint character? You can tell this by going back and reading the last chapter with this character in it. You can't imagine how many authors, ourselves included, forget that in the last chapter, Phil had a gun pointed at his head. We get up the next day and try to write a new scene. Regardless of whether it is a day later or ten years later, Phil needs to start by thinking about how he felt with that gun pressed against his head. Then, Phil decides what he wants to do now. That decision is his transition to a new scene with him as protagonist.

Maybe Phil didn't have a gun pressed against his head. Maybe he had Natalie's lips pressed against his lips. Different emotion, same situation. What does Phil feel when we return to his viewpoint?

Repeat, the accelerator is emotion. Before you begin your transition, locate the emotion. One word. Write it down. Phil's primary emotion is...

The brake is pace. Your pace keeps you from moving too fast, but it can also slow you to a stop. In transition, there's no dialogue. Thus, the pace is far slower than a scene with dialogue and conflict. A paragraph of transition moves slower than two pages of dialogue. You must keep it short.

Wait, you might say. *Isn't that telling?*

Yes.

Didn't you say we're supposed to show, not tell?

That's right.

Nasty sneer. *Then why the switch?*

Because a transition is not a scene. It's a device that connects your scenes and keeps them from being episodic.

Everything in writing is a choice. If you simply went

through your day and wrote down everything you did, you'd have a minutia-laden journal. Fiction writers get to choose what to record, and in the digital age, we need to seriously consider our choices. Which are your big-stake scenes? Play them out from moment to moment. What are your tooth-brushing, telephone-talking dreaded events? Paraphrase them.

Once you locate your character's emotion from the last scene he was in, it's time to move to reflection.

Your protagonist—let's call him Hank—meets Jenny, the woman of his dreams. They spend a night together, and he wakes up alone.

"Jenny," he calls out. "Jenny, where are you?"

No one answers. The woman he just fell in love with is gone.

End of scene.

Now you have to ask yourself what the next scene should be. Should it be your protagonist trying to find Jenny, visiting her apartment or the office where she told him she works? Should it be months or years later when he has a hint about what may have happened to cause her to leave that night? Should it be a day he is getting ready to marry a woman who looks like Jenny? A mountain of possibilities. How do you mine them? You begin with emotion and then reflection, which lead you to action, and that's how you organically move into your next scene. In all three examples, let's make the primary emotion frustration.

Reflection #1

He thought about Jenny all day. No way could she disappear. The apartment he thought was hers was occupied by an old couple who told him they'd been there for three years. The office where he'd picked her up was deserted. As he walked the dark streets that night, he reached in his pocket and realized the key she'd given him was still there. He pulled it out and studied the numerals on it. An address. It was late, but he didn't care. He'd beat down the door if he had to.

Reflection #2

Some nights he still thought about Jenny, but after three years, his feelings for her had hardened into anger. After failing to locate her, he'd gotten involved with other women, but those relationships always ended the same way—with him being unable to commit. On the morning after Stacy walked out, he knew he couldn't keep pretending. He needed to finish what he had started with Jenny once and for all.

Reflection #3

He'd learned since that night Jenny had disappeared how to shut off his emotions. Sure, he'd tried to find her, but once it was clear that she and no one else had planned her disappearance, he allowed himself to pretend she never mattered. By tomorrow, he and Kara would be married and on the Hawaiian honeymoon paid for by Kara's very rich father. Except that something was wrong. Jenny had mentioned a sister who lived on Maui. He needed to go to Hawaii, all right, but he had to go there alone.

Regardless of which outcome you select, it will lead you to your character's next scene goal. That's how powerful this tool is. Use it correctly, and you won't have to worry about your plot. Nor will you have to worry about episodic fiction.

Of course, you won't need transitions for every scene. Many will be implied. However, the next time you're wondering how you're going to move from one scene to another, you have a way to do so.

Speaking of transition, it's time to advance to the big picture. You know how to construct a scene, with all of its dynamic and intricate parts. Character. POV. Backstory. Dialogue. You also understand how to glue those scenes together with transition. Now, it's time to inspect your novel as a whole. Not the individual pieces any more, but the big story, which means we're going to need a huge, solid hook.

CHAPTER TEN

THE BIG HOOK: FISHING FOR *JAWS*

Now that we've gotten through the basics, it's time to step back and look at the big picture, which includes how the digital age relates to your writing. We've already said that the publishing industry has changed forever. With the invention of the Kindle and Nook, smart phones, Apple, and other devices, endless worldwide distribution is available to any author with a manuscript and a dream.

Remember drunk Uncle Bob and his guide to hitting on college women? He's polishing up his third manuscript as we speak. Today's readers are flooded with choices and drenched in content.

Technology guru and innovator Mitchell Kapor said, "Getting information off the Internet is like taking a drink from a fire hydrant."

This applies to all digital information, e-books included. These days, many novels aren't vetted by agents and editors, or anyone for that matter. What we are left with is millions of manuscripts flittering before the eyes of potential readers, who have very few ways to tell the difference between J.K. Rowling and Uncle Bob.

Published authors are not exempt from this phenomenon either. We have to fish for readers in the exact same ocean as everyone else. If you expect these fish to jump willingly into your schooner, think again. They're hungry, busy, overwhelmed, and moving fast. Authors today might as well be fishing for *Jaws*.

Needless to say, we're all going to need a bigger boat, or net, or at least better craft.

With so much competition in the digital age, an author's skill matters more than ever, because any reader can download a sample chapter of your book from the comfort of her home. If she doesn't like your writing, you will be deleted. Believe us, millions of other authors are waiting to take your place.

Therefore, you have to hook your reader quickly if you expect her to click the buy button. As we explained back in Chapter Five, the best way to grab the reader is by introducing conflict in each scene.

Why do you think drivers gawk at car accidents on the side of the road? For better or worse, people don't like unresolved conflict. Is anyone hurt? Will the driver live? Of course it's dangerous to rubberneck, but we can't help ourselves because the question has latched into our brain and yanked our head. If you want to hook the modern reader, you need to do the same thing on the page. This is no small task.

Author and writing instructor Jack Bickham wrote, "Readers today are more hurried and impatient—and jaded by swiftly paced television drama; they want condensation, speed, and punch."

Now think about this. That quote from Bickham's writing book, *Scene And Structure*, was published in 1993, well before the jump edits in Hollywood movies pulsed like strobe lights. In order to apply his words today, magnify their meaning by several orders of magnitude.

In your writing arsenal, you have dozens of spears and hooks. A strong opening line and a compelling voice always help, but there is one harpoon that's best suited to snare your reader in the first few pages and pull him to the last.

Story goal. You need to reveal it in the first chapter, but what is it?

True, every scene in your book needs a protagonist with a goal. Every scene also needs somebody to stand in her way. This is the essence of scene. Remember, I want A, and you want B.

In addition, your novel as a whole needs an overarching story goal. Some authors called it story question, because it can be posed in the form of a question.

Suzanne Collins didn't waste time getting to the story goal when she wrote *The Hunger Games*. Will Katniss Everdeen survive the Hunger Games? We readers hear about the reaping for the games in the first paragraph. Brilliant.

If your story goal is the main problem of your novel, it definitely needs to be resolved when you reach the end of the book. Just like each scene goal, your story goal has an answer, which should be *yes* or *no*. Early on, it's your best chance to hook the reader. Think about your manuscript. What's your story goal?

To be clear, your characters are hands down the strongest hooks your novel can have, but they take many chapters to develop properly. Your story goal needs only a sentence and a good setup, and it will lodge into your reader's brain and pull her along until she relates to your characters. At that point, she's onboard.

When you present your novel's story goal in the first chapter, you not only work to hook the reader, but you'll also avoid a plot that floats along aimlessly. If your reader knows the main problem and the stakes early on, she'll have a harder time putting your book down. That translates to her clicking the buy button, which brings her one step closer to becoming the ravenous great white shark that hungers for your books.

CHAPTER ELEVEN

THE PROBLEM WITH PLOT

Are you feeling the strain of the mid-novel hump? Here you are, six months and forty thousand words into your manuscript, and just when your plot really needs to ramp up, you find that it stagnates. Your outline makes sense in your handwritten notes or even in your head, but no matter what you try, the story just won't move forward. Or maybe, like many authors, you just don't know where to go next.

If you're having plot problems, welcome to the vast wasteland where mediocre novels go to die. Sounds bad, we know, but before you fill your jacket pockets with stones and walk into a lake Virginia Woolf-style, let's get to the good news.

Every author deals with plot problems. You are not alone. That's why it's so important to have a plan to deal with the plot issues when they inevitably arise. Rest assured, these plot speed bumps are an easy fix when you realize that they are actually character problems in disguise. Strong characters leap into action. They have clearly defined goals, which naturally lead to new obstacles. Think about it. Harry Potter doesn't dither. The minute any of his friends are in danger, he steps in to protect them.

If plotting is a dance between your protagonist and antagonist, it only makes sense that you'll find the solutions to your problems in that dance, and therefore, in those characters who are dancing. So instead of listening to your inner demons when they whisper that this book is hopeless, take a second to appreciate plot problems for what they really are—that is, opportunities to adjust and strengthen your characters.

Let's take a look at an example.

Back in Chapter Five, we showed that great fiction has conflict on every page. Again, this is not to imply a fistfight on every page, just two characters with differing goals.

For the sake of lunacy, let's say that you've written a book about a chef named Doreen, who for some awful reason wants to cook liver and onions for dinner. It's a vile creation, we agree, but it's only here to illustrate our point. Now, let's say that our scene antagonist Bob adores liver and onions. Here, you've painted a scenario where the conflict, and therefore, the plot tension will disintegrate faster than that nasty liver in Bob's mouth.

How about something more serious? Doreen and Bob are trapped on an island with a killer. During their escape, they come across a boat.

If Doreen is an expert sailor, and Bob spent his youth on fishing boats in Alaska, you suffer the same lack of conflict as the liver example above. Naturally, Doreen and Bob will both want to hop on that boat and head to safety. Again, your tension will stagnate despite the crazed murderer chasing them, and you the author, have missed an important opportunity for your characters to grow.

These types of non-conflict scenarios cause your plot to drag. In fact, a slumping plot is always caused by one of two flaws.

- Weak characters who don't push the story

forward.
• A lack of conflict (which is based on character).

Either way, we're back to character problems. Some authors know that they need conflict, so when faced with situations like these, they try to invent conflict with a nasty argument, or worse, the dreaded fistfight we mentioned earlier.

Creating conflict from nothing is possibly the worst sin any novelist can commit, and for sure it is the most damaging. Good authors guide their stories forward, and develop their characters to deal with issues that arise. Forcing your characters to behave in ways they never would in real life in order to advance the plot is a guaranteed way to lose readers.

Why is that? When your character's behavior is illogical, a splinter of disbelief breaks off in the reader's mind. Those splinters plant seeds on a deep level that the reader is being lied to. What truths can anyone possibly take away from a dishonest author? Worse yet, in the age where false advertisements fill every space of our lives— even the computers and TVs in our homes—people will turn off and tune out at the slightest hint of dishonesty. Your novel is no exception. So how do you deal honestly with plot problems? The best method is by investigating the characters in your scenes and allowing for their growth throughout the book. Can you say that you knew no more about your protagonist at the end than you did on page one? We hope not.

So your initial knowledge of Bob wasn't entirely accurate. Sure, he spent his college summers working for the fishing industry, but maybe he suffered a terrible accident where he nearly died at sea. Not only is that plausible, but it's probable, considering the nature of the profession. Furthermore, that type of tragedy could drive Sponge Bob to fear the sea.

So maybe Bob is now hydrophobic, and we have a situation where he will do anything to avoid the water. Doreen's plan to escape the killer involves the boat. Bob may feel more comfortable making their stand on the beach.

Both characters now have a bigger interest in the outcome of your scene. The stakes have been raised, and even you, the author, may not know which way your plot will head next. The outcome of this plot speed bump has not only opened your mind to new directions, but it has strengthened your understanding of Bob as well.

Better yet, when you allow your characters to grow in response to other characters or external stimuli in the story, the overall effect is natural and organic. It feels truthful to the reader, and the origins of Bob's fear of water come out in relation to the events happening around him.

Readers can relate to him because the revelations won't seem forced either. That's how all people begin to change, isn't it? By interacting with other people. And the details of his condition will seep out in dialogue and in his actions, instead of the dreaded inner monologue.

So in the end, your characters must be fluid and malleable. Rigidity is Kryptonite for any artist, but especially for authors. You don't have to worry about plot problems. When you create great characters and listen to them, give them room to breathe, they will reward you with intriguing plot twists that will keep the reader turning those pages.

CHAPTER TWELVE

THE EDITING FAIRY: THAT WOULD BE YOU

So here we are, approaching the close of this guided tour. Whether you're a traditionalist seeking agent representation or a free-spirited self-publisher choosing to pirate the high seas alone, this guide will serve as your map through these turbulent times of the e-book explosion. Either path is respectable. Each has its advantages and shortcomings. It's up to you to decide what makes the most sense for your career. Whichever road you choose, you need to take a crucial piece of information with you on your journey.

There is no editing fairy.

It's horrible to tell authors such things, we know, especially those who believe with all their heart, but we have to rip that Band-Aid off sometime. Tinker Bell is not going to fly down from Neverland to wave her magic wand over your manuscript to fix all of the craft and punctuation glitches that you've certainly accumulated.

Sure, a great agent might help you see the flaws, but in order to receive her wonderful input, you have to land her first. How interested do you think she'll be in a manuscript that's riddled with punctuation errors?

Self-publishers have even more responsibility because no professional editor or agent will be heading the clean-up effort. Readers will tolerate an error or two. Maybe three.

After that, you fall into the pit of amateurs. That's the desolate, frigid region, where lost souls waste unthinkable amounts of energy and money on promotion because they didn't bother to learn the difference between *your* and *you're*. Don't end up in that pit of despair. Make sure your manuscript is clean before you even think about publishing.

The good news is that most of these glitches are easy to fix. Here are the most common copy mistakes to watch out for in your manuscript.

Punctuation crutches

When we're unsure about the strength of our writing, we often lean on punctuation and formatting to hit our message home. Unfortunately, these tools cannot salvage weak prose. They only draw attention to it.

Colons and semicolons add a scholarly tone that may sound archaic in your novel. Furthermore, they will flatten your pace. In dialogue, they violate point-of-view as most of us do not think or listen with semicolons in mind. We speak and listen with our emotions.

Ellipses...well...they really do slow your pace...believe us on that one. Besides, they do not substitute for dashes or periods. They're meant to indicate missing words from a quotation. You can also use them to show that the character is interrupted in mid-speech. Be careful though. Every sentence can't trail off into a haze of dot-dot-dots. Too many probably indicate that you're relying on punctuation to prop up your writing.

A major problem with punctuation crutches is that they travel in packs. Show us one semicolon on a page of your book, and we'll show you a colony. The same is true with one of the most abused punctuation marks on the planet. You know what we're talking about, don't you?

Exclamation points. These poor creatures get tacked at the end of any sentence that can't stand on its own. F. Scott Fitzgerald said, "An exclamation point is like laughing at your own joke."

He's right. Use them rarely, if ever.

"But how will the reader know that my character really means it?" you may ask. Make your language strong enough to stand on its own.

"Get your stinking paws off me, you damn dirty ape," Charlton Heston said. No need for extra punctuation. The dialogue's meaning is clear, even on the page.

We mentioned traveling in packs. "Don't you ever use more than one exclamation point!!!!!!!! Are we clear?!!!"

Not in dialogue. Not in exposition. Not ever. Pass the Excedrin.

Also related to this phenomenon, is our friend, Mr. Caps Lock.

"YOU STAY AWAY FROM ME," she shouted.

That type of behavior is fine for Facebook, but it has no place in fiction. Come to think of it, don't do it on Facebook either.

Adverbs, adjectives, and no-shit Sherlocks.

Stephen King nailed one part of this problem when he said, "The road to hell is paved with adverbs." Cut them wherever you can, or replace the weak verb that they're modifying. If your protagonist *walked quickly*, the correct verb might be *ran* or *jogged*. If he *spoke loudly*, *yelled* or *shouted* works better.

Adjectives can be equally redundant. The worst are the dark-and-stormy night variety. *Jane was sad and depressed. She should have been grateful and optimistic.* You get the idea. We're using two words dark-and-stormy style here because we sense unconsciously that neither is strong enough to satisfy the reader. Keep searching. Better yet, put yourself in your character's head. *Jane felt like throwing herself out the window.*

You also need to check for what we call no-shit Sherlocks. That is: *He wrapped his fingers around Jane's throat. She was terrified.* No need to tell us that last part. We get it.

When you're in the heat of a first draft, you'll find yourself tossing around adverbs, adjectives, and no-shit Sherlocks like confetti. That's exactly what you should be doing in the first draft. Remember, you can fix anything but a blank page, but eventually you do need to fix it.

Very and the really, reallys. You really have to understand why this section is very, very important. Really, this section falls under unnecessary adjectives and adverbs that really slow down your pace. Look at the alternative.

You have to understand why this section is important. See the difference. It appears as though an adult wrote it and not a fourth-grader, but don't take it from us.

Mark Twain said it best. "Substitute 'damn' every time you're inclined to write "very." Your editor will delete it and the writing will be just as it should be."

That's one smart man.

Echoes. These delightful little gems have a tendency to pop up when we're not thinking about them, like when Pops used to make pop-tarts for you. Echoes draw attention to themselves and can cause the reader to wake from your story. As authors, our goal should be to use most words once—not just in the same paragraph, but also on the entire page if possible.

He-hes and the she-shes. This is an extension of the echoed words theory. When you have too much action and exposition in a scene with no conflict, the he-hes nest and breed a rash of boring pronouns. For instance:

John walked across the street to the liquor store. What he really needed was some chewing gum. He pulled out his wad of ones and he paid the clerk. He then walked back to his vehicle. That's when he saw Tom.

The he-he's show up when we don't take the time to set up our scenes properly. Notice that John is walking and buying and chewing all alone. If all of these actions are absolutely necessary, you should shorten them. Then find a way to get into your next scene.

John walked over to the liquor store, bought a pack of gum, and met Tom and his partner Gus outside.

"We need to go," he said.

"We're not done here yet." Tom motioned to Gus, whose chest was as big as a truck tire. "We'll leave when I say so."

John wants to leave. A. Tom wants to stay. B. Notice that there aren't any he-hes.

High-impact words and phrases. These words and images punch the reader like rifle slugs. Whenever possible, you should always replace limp words with their high-octane counterpart. Punch. Slugs. Octane. Limp. See what we mean?

Blade is a lovely word, but an X-Acto knife conjures a stronger image. Sure, your character may need new bandages, but that doesn't mean you need to describe it in that way. Instead, blood might seep through his gauze pad. Or maybe, that nameless celebrity host on television should be called by his name, Alex Trebec. Did the couple drink wine or chardonnay? Was the flower fragrant, or did the carnation smell like exotic spice? Is that rain you're describing a sprinkle or a thunderstorm? Is that man on the street a thug, a surfer in a wetsuit, or an overage jock huffing and puffing? The more specific your language—filtered through your point-of-view character, of course—the more real your setting.

Remember, these high-impact words and names create such vivid mental images, that one shot is enough. The first echo of one of these words waters down its power and draws too much attention. Your reader will realize that she's reading. Bad author. Big mistake.

The Old Words Home. Some words and phrases are just too old. William Saroyan could use "commenced" and did so frequently. Not such a great idea today. If you still do, send it to the Old Words Home, the place where tired words and phrases go to live out the rest of their lives. Don't worry. They'll have nurses and shuffleboard, and you won't have to deal with those words in your writing.

Clichés also need to get out of your writing and into the home. The word, cliché, a nineteenth-century French term, refers to a printing plate that was used after the original plate wore out. And plates wore out, of course, because they were overused. Language is no different. Even if your character is cool as a cucumber, and ready to give the devil his due, you have the chops to kick it to the curb and come up with something fresh as a daisy. Well, maybe not, but you get the idea. The first author who described someone's eyes as *jade green* might have been original, but the term should now be retired. *Silken loins* might have been sexy once, but it sounds like something at a butcher shop and it's been used too many times to conjure a fresh image in the reader.

Comic book sounds need a one-way ticket to the home too.

BAM! POW! BANG! CRASH!

"Gosh, Robin, the reader has ears. Maybe he already knows how something sounds."

"Yeah, Batman, but when I was a kid and pretended to shoot a gun, I made a noise in my mouth, mostly spit, that sounded like "PITTEW!"

"Ew. Got it, Robin. Let's wipe off our faces and send that one right to the Old Words Home."

We use these tired old words and phrases when we're on a roll and the story is flowing, and that's fine. At that moment, you just need to slam those words on the page. When you re-read your manuscript in edit mode (and only once you've finished the first draft), you need to move past the cliché place-holder to what you really meant. That's what the second, third, and fourth drafts are for. In those editing sweeps, you need to also look out for content glitches. The next chapter will show you how.

CHAPTER THIRTEEN

BEYOND SPELLCHECK: EDITING FOR CONTENT ERRORS

Editing your manuscript requires more than running your grammar-check software. Surely you've experienced that nightmare. Semicolons replace commas. Weird sentence constructions obliterate your prose. Even if you are confident that you've caught every comma and rescued every misplaced modifier, you need to weed out the content errors that will harm your novel and make you sound like an amateur. These are not problems with language; they are problems with your story.

You're the protagonist.
Your name is Robert Dennis Smith. You name your character Dennis Roberts. Your name is Joyce. You name your character JJ, and you have her driving that red Corvette you always wanted to own. If you have a child, so does JJ. If you have six children, so does she. How can you expect to achieve honesty on the page when you've already trapped your story within the walls of your own life? We confess. We've done it. And it didn't work for us any more than it's going to work for you.

But that's what really happened.
This is closely related to naming the character after you. Instead, you've created an imaginary character and

limited how she can respond to the conflicts in her environment. Janie gets it on with her best friend's husband in the men's room at the company Christmas party. That leaves Janie unsympathetic and not even empathetic. *Hey, author. Why did your character do this with her best friend's husband?*

Beady little eye gleam. *"Because,"* the author says, *"That's what I did with my friend's husband."*

You can't rip events from your life and slam them on the page just because they happened. If you are still doing this, get therapy, if only to save your writing.

The Page-142 Syndrome.

Yes, your pace is a little slow, but that's only because you have a great deal to share about your protagonist. Thus, he not only circles the airport and thinks about his life in Chapter One. He then jumps in a rental car and drives to Ensenada, still thinking about his life. *Hey, writer, where's the dialogue?*

"Just wait," you say. *"Once you get to page 142, the story really takes off."*

If it really takes off on page 142, start it there.

Researchitis.

This dreaded disease inflicts authors with the compulsion to impart every smidgeon of useless information uncovered while researching their novels. You research how bees make honey. You research how to make a chocolate soufflé or become an expert pole dancer. Once you've completed all of the research, you want to share every detail. Don't. Spewing every research fact on the page is actually just a way to prove how smart you are. Remember, this book is about your characters. Not you.

Researchitis gives you a deadly slow pace, which gives your reader a reason to put the book down.

Fruitcake.
Do you look forward to eating that fruitcake your Aunt Madge brings over every Christmas? Didn't think so. Is your prose so sweet and rich and laden with greasy nuts that it sends readers into mental image overload? If you have large sections of exposition and descriptions without dialogue, you may be in fruitcake mode. Trash that baby and cut to the chase.

Word packages.
Some people go through their lives speaking in word packages.

"How are you, Antonia?"

"Fine, Vic. I'm fine."

"How was your weekend?"

"Fabulous. How was yours?"

"It was a lot of fun. I shot my mother-in-law and left her body on the stairs."

"Cool, Vic. Talk to you soon. Take care."

Antonia is not engaged in this conversation. She is speaking in word packages in order to avoid connecting with Vic or anyone else, and most of all, herself. She's memorized the prompts, and she may be able to get through an entire day without ever noticing that Vic is burying family members in her backyard.

"Hey Antonia, can I borrow your hacksaw?"

"Not a problem, Vic."

"Would you mind putting your fingerprints on it first?"

"Sure thing."

Authors who rely on meaningless word packages in real life are seldom able to break free of them when they write fiction. Thus, they may end up with: *"It was an upscale neighborhood with manicured lawns." "He walked the two short blocks to the apartment." "She was an ebony-haired beauty."* How many millions of times have you read such descriptions? Do they allow you to see or feel anything fresh? Of course not. It's fine to use them for placeholders on the first draft, but if you want to connect with your reader, eventually you need to edit those packages out of your manuscript.

"So I can't just go with my first draft?"

Afraid not. In fact, you should probably give your novel time to breathe so that you can be more objective about its flaws. To paraphrase poet Archibald MacLeish, the first draft needs to sit like apples in a drawer. In a day or a few days, you can decide whether or not those apples are rotten or ripe.

Remember, even with the best-trained eye, most novels require seven or eight sweeps to find all of the problems that normally occur. Whether you're searching for an agent or you're going the self-publishing route, you need to learn to recognize these glitches on the page.

Even if you plan on paying an editor to clean your manuscript, it's not enough. For one thing, you self-publishers out there should know that real editors are expensive. We're not talking about your sister the English teacher here. Five thousand for a professional edit is not out of the question. Some charge more. That money can be spent in other places, such as setting up book signings in different cities or purchasing your Facebook and Google ads.

Editors operate like battlefield surgeons. If your novel is too problematic, they'll begin fixing only what's necessary to keep it alive. Forget the fact that an iron lung is poking through the gaping hole in its chest. At least it's breathing. Doesn't that make sense too? If every sentence has some problem in it, they have to rewrite the whole novel. That could be months of intensive work, and we authors aren't always the easiest lot to deal with.

If you're serious about your writing career, take the time to learn punctuation and the mechanics of craft. Once you know what to look for, it isn't difficult. You'll save money, and your writing will be stronger. That way, if an editor does sit down with your manuscript, she can fix the right things and send you out into the world with a professional novel to promote.

CHAPTER FOURTEEN

HUBRIS: THE FATAL FLAW

At the beginning of this book, we warned you that anybody who can write a grocery list is now writing and publishing novels. Great authors and terrible authors share the same virtual bookshelf. You have already learned how to compete with the greats and outshine the rest, and no one can stop you, except yourself.

So what's next? Assuming that you've listened to at least most of what we've had to say about craft, is there a message to sum up how to build a writing career for the instant-gratification generation?

There is no need for a "You can do it," rally-the-troops, *Braveheart* speech now, because—let's be honest—those speeches are usually a precursor to sending out soldiers for slaughter. We have higher hopes for you. But we do have one final message that encompasses everything you need to know about writing fiction in the digital age.

Beware of hubris.

Hubris: the greatest crime in ancient Greek mythology, extreme haughtiness, pride or arrogance. Since the beginning of civilization, it has plagued human society. Just ask the Greeks, who warned against it endlessly in their stories. Oedipus, Antigone, Medea. Their outcomes are as tragic as the egos of the protagonists.

You know what's changed since ancient times?

Nothing. In fact, modern society is fueled by excessive pride, whether it's deserved or not. Make no mistake, when this civilization collapses, leaving nothing among the ruins except a few Kindles with photos of Richard Wright or Emily Dickenson still etched onto the cracked screens, it will be because of that same pride.

Vanity. Ego. Arrogance. Call it what you like, but these traits will ruin your manuscript if you're not careful. We're not talking about your characters. We're talking about you. Without a doubt, the most common reason an author fails is hubris.

That's what William Faulkner meant when he gave the excellent advice, "Kill your darlings." As you probably know, a darling is something you put in the book because you love it. If you love it, you can't be objective about it. You really did think it would be fun to use your ex as the protagonist and expose all of the times that jerk cheated on you. Except darlings are almost always too obvious. You need to be able to explore your fictional protagonist without that baggage. Kill the darling, and start with a fresh protagonist.

Darlings aren't just characters. The one you love could be a certain phrase or stark description you are certain makes you sound deep and literary. Nevertheless, it's got to go too. The inability to kill it or any other darling because you are convinced it is pure genius is a sign of hubris.

When we are speaking about craft at conferences, someone inevitably suffers a meltdown.

"What about Moby Dick?" he demands. "Melville didn't pay attention to any point-of-view rules."

As much as we appreciate the classics—and we do—using any great book as an attempt to excuse your own inadequacies as a writer is unrealistic.

In reality, these Moby Dickers are really saying, "You don't know what you're talking about, because my book is already written, and I'm not going to change anything."

May we suggest Darlings Anonymous?

The "But Danielle Steel Does It" Syndrome.
This is a variation on the Moby Dickers.

"Well, you said I needed a consistent point-of-view in this scene. But, as you can see right here, Danielle Steel is writing in the point-of-view of the poodle on the sidewalk as he looks up at the beautiful woman."

For some odd reason, Melville and Steel are the most quoted of those who desperately seek excuses to avoid changing their fiction. Instead of trying to fix what doesn't work in their manuscripts, the Dickers and the Steelers dig through a bunch of old books, highlighter pen in hand, so that they can say to you, and more important, to themselves, *I was right, after all. I was right.*

More power to them. This is the digital age, where the reach of your iMac, magnified by the Internet, can be seductive. Don't want to take constructive criticism? Don't have to. Publish direct to Kindle on your own terms today. You don't even have to worry about readers ripping you to shreds. After all, they have to buy the book before they're allowed to leave a comment. They won't get that far.

Are you allowing your ego to decide what to change in your manuscript and what to retain? Here are the most common ego-driven errors to avoid.

The Great Style Lie.
Oh, what's wrong? Do you really love your meandering point-of-view, your fragments, and your numerous word packages?

"It's my style. Can't change it. Never could. Not ever. Not especially when I think about it. And I'm thinking now. Thinking."

Really? So you're comfortable with fragments that might have looked fresh back in Kerouac's day?

"I already told you. It's my style. And enough already about Kerouac."

Styles are flexible. Hubris is not. Why do you refuse to retire those dreary old words and structures? Don't bother to answer. We already know.

Refusing to read.

Writers who admit they don't read have two excuses, both flawed. One type says, "I don't read because I don't want to let any of the books I read influence my style." You don't want to be influenced by brilliant writers, because...? You're afraid the brilliance might rub off on you? Do you really think reading Hemingway, Didion, or Raymond Carver will turn you into a copy of that person? If only.

The other reason some writers refuse to read is this. "I don't read. I watch movies. They are stories, after all." They sure are, and they offer you an escape from watching how words play out on the page. When you watch a story on the screen—and we love to do that as much as you do—you may learn how to hone dialogue, but that's about it. Again, writing fiction isn't about watching a movie from a seat in the audience. It's about being the movie.

Honesty.

For whatever reason, some writers have never dealt with their lives honestly. You're jealous of the sister you pretend is your best friend. You rationalize the fact that Mommy abused you. She worked two jobs to put clothes on your back, after all. You may even use drugs or alcohol to numb your thoughts and disappointments. You are the one who will write pages of prose with no conflict—because you can't bear to look at the personal conflict threatening to implode in your own life.

You believe writing will free you. The dream of being a writer is the bright sun above that dark hole of your life. Until you can look away from the sun and study yourself, including the darker parts, you cannot begin to create honest characters. Writing isn't an escape. It's a life's work and passion.

If you recognize yourself in any of the statements above, consider why you are still clinging to these flawed darlings. Could it be hubris? If so, just know that it is a poisonous injection, mainlined into the vein of your career. To make matters worse, we live in a world governed by it. Hubris will hamper your ability to take advice and recognize honest feedback when you hear it. Instead, it will convince you that you were born with the writer's gene, and nothing can improve your brilliant prose.

Alas, there is no gene. Without fail, the writers who succeed certainly were not bestowed the magical mark of the author's quill at birth. They worked hard. They used criticism to improve, overcame rejection, and sought out every opportunity to improve their craft.

You can succeed too. You have all the necessary tools. This writing world is yours to take, if you want it. So dig in. Read. Write. Every day. Learn from your victories. Learn from your mistakes. You are the author who knows that marketing is no substitute for hard work. You are not rigid, prideful, or lazy. Go out into the digital age, armed with the skill of craft, and we promise you can begin to build the brilliant writing career that you have in you.

Now quit reading this. Go write. Your readers are waiting.

ABOUT THE AUTHORS

Joe Osejo Photography

Bonnie Hearn Hill is the author of six thrillers, four young adult novels, and numerous nonfiction titles. A former newspaper editor, she writes articles on the craft of writing and leads online and real time workshops.

Christopher Allan Poe is an author and touring musician from Los Angeles. He writes paranormal fiction, with an emphasis on social issues involving women and children. He has been accepted into the International Thriller Writers Debut Authors Program.

Bonnie and Christopher speak at conferences across the country, and they love hearing from writers. Contact them through their website at:

www.DIGITALINKBOOKS.com

CPSIA information can be obtained
at www.ICGtesting.com
Printed in the USA
LVOW13s0109270717

542811LV00011B/75/P